Elizabeth Ficken's deep knowledge and love for the Bible shines through in each of her in-depth studies. Using her gifts of teaching and diving deep into God's Word, Elizabeth has taken the familiar passages and teaching of John 14, 15, and 16 and brings a new level of richness and understanding to them. This study will help any woman desiring a deeper understanding of God's Word to see more clearly the love and promises of God in this precious message from Jesus.
— *Chrissy Morton, Former CRU Missionary Intern, Women's Bible Study leader, wife, mother of 3, The Shepherd's Church, Cary, NC*

Having enthusiastically employed Elizabeth Ficken's *Letters to the Thessalonians* study in our church's Women's Ministry, I am delighted to endorse *Abide in Me*. With extensive research and engaging explanations of the text, Elizabeth not only expertly and expositionally guides the minds of women eager to plumb the depths of God's Word, but she also passionately exhorts sisters to pray for and share the joy of discovering true and everlasting love in Christ, supernatural dependence on the power of Holy Spirit, and our sure hope of heaven from God the Father in the midst of earthly sorrows - so needed for every believer!
— *Tracy Lee, Women's Ministry Leader, Pastor's wife, Rooted Church, a multi-ethnic church, Cary, NC*

Devotion & Dependence

on Jesus Christ

An in-depth Bible study of John 14 - 16

Elizabeth Bagwell Ficken

Abide in Me: Devotion and Dependence on Jesus Christ © Copyright 2023
by Elizabeth Bagwell Ficken
Printed in the United States of America
W & E Publishing, Cary, NC

Scripture quotations identified as NKJV are from the Holy Bible,
New King James Version, copyright © 1979, 1980, 1982, Thomas Nelson, Inc.
Publishers. Used by permission. All rights reserved.

Scripture quotations identified NASB are from the
New American Standard Bible © The Lockman Foundation, 1960, 1962, 1963,
1968, 1971, 1972, 1973, 1975, 1977. Used by permission.

Scripture quotations identified NIV are from the *New International Version*,
copyright © 1973, 1978, 1984 by International Bible Society.

Scripture quotations identified NLT are from the Holy Bible,
New Living Translation, copyright © 1996. Used by permission of
Tyndale House Publisher, Inc., Wheaton, Illionois 60189. All rights reserved.

Scripture quotations identified ESV are from The Holy Bible, *English Standard Version*® (ESV®), copyright ©2001 by Crossway Bibles, a publishing ministry of
Good News Publishers. Used by permission. All rights reserved.

Scripture quotations identfied HCSB are from the *Holman Christian Standard Bible*®, Copyright 1999, 2000, 2002, 2003, 2009 by Holman Bible Publishers. Used
by permission. Holman Christian Stand Bible®, Holman CSB®, and HCSB® are
federally registered trademarks of Holman Bible Publishers.

Scripture quotations identified as NET are from *The NET Bible*®
Copyright © 2005 by Biblical Studies Press, L.L.C. www.bible.org.
All rights reserved.

"Do you know Jesus?" Gospel presentation from Sonlife Classic.
Copyright © 2009 Used by permission.

Cover: Jeannine Klingbeil

This book is dedicated with love and respect to my father, George E. Bagwell III. He abides in Christ, lives by the power of the Holy Spirit and bears much fruit.

I am the vine, you are the branches.
He who abides in Me, and I in him, bears much fruit;
for without Me you can do nothing.
John 15:5 [NKJ]

ISBN– 978-0-9905933-9-3

Table of Contents

Foreword		7
Introduction		9
My Bible Story		10
Do You Know Jesus?		11
Helpful Hints		12
Lessons:		
1. A View from Above	John's Gospel	15
2. An Exclusive Meeting	John 13:31-16:33	19
3. The Plan	John 13:31-38	24
4. Trust Me	John 14:1-6	27
5. The Need to Know	John 14:6-14	32
6. It's All About Love	John 14:15-26	36
7. His Gift of Peace	John 14:27-31	42
8. The Vinedresser and the Vineyard	John 15:1-6	46
9. An Abundant Harvest	John 15:1-17	50
10. The Valuable Vine	John 15:8-17	55
11. Bad News	John 15:18-25	59
12. Good Works	John 15:26-16:7	64
13. The Work of the Holy Spirit	John 16:8-15	68
14. A Time of Sorrow	John 16:16-22	72
15. Ask the Father	John 16:22-28	76
16. Never Alone	John 16:29-33	80
17. Be of Good Cheer!	John 16:33	84
18. Our Inheritance	John 13:31-16:33	90
Endnotes		92
Suggested Books and Commentaries		94
Prayer Requests and Praises		96-107
Other In-depth Bible Studies by Elizabeth Bagwell Ficken		108
Information on free resources at elizabethficken.com		110

Foreword

My mother is a Bible teacher. Before she started writing studies, before she attended seminary, she was teaching the Bible. I know she was teaching before she even had me, but I can only speak to the days, months, years that I was one of her primary students. If she had just read something interesting, she would pull out a Bible at the kitchen table to tell us about it. If we were on the way home from church, she would turn around from the passenger seat to help expound, explain, and discuss the sermon.

If I had to pick one word that wove through all her teaching, year after year as she studied and grew and wrote and taught, it would be "abide." This word in particular, and this word nestled in the context of John 15, seemed to connect to every lesson she shared with me. There is no denying what this scripture means to her. It comes out in every context of her life, most importantly in the way that she lives. She abides in Christ.

John 14-16 is a personal, intimate address from Jesus to His disciples. This is His final teaching and final preparation for His disciples who have followed and trusted Him throughout His ministry. Who will help them in His absence? What does following the commands of Jesus really mean for their lives? What hope does Jesus give them right before He departs? What does "abide" even mean?

Because my mother cares so deeply about these chapters and truths, she handles them with reverence and weight. I trust her own devotion and dependence on Jesus Christ, so be assured that she is a well-equipped guide as you journey with her through the words of Jesus.

— Emily Nelsen, Bible study author and teacher, The Summit Church, Apex, NC

Introduction

Dear Friends,

I've been enjoying writing in-depth Bible studies for about 20 years. Each one has been on a whole book of the Bible, and every new study has added a new book to my list of favorites. I've enjoyed writing on New Testament letters, and the gospel of Matthew, and Old Testament prophecies, psalms and Job's poetic suffering.

Over the years, my father regularly urged me to write on his favorite book, the gospel of John. To which I regularly replied — I've already written a study on the gospel of Matthew! However, I had John 15 on my favorites list and hoped that one day I would write a study on that beautiful chapter.

Here it is! This study is a result of wanting to honor my father's request as well as fulfilling my own heart's desire to share the intimate teaching of John 15. Because of the importance of understanding the context of verses and passages, and because of my awareness of the critical teaching found only in John 14 and 16, the Lord led me to write this in-depth study of the last message of Jesus to His disciples which was recorded by the beloved disciple John.

Even though John 15 has been a very special chapter to me for many years, studying the whole message of Jesus has been enlightening. I am delighting in John 14, 15, 16, and am very excited to share these chapters with you!

That's my story of how I came to write this Bible study. But my story isn't that important. What is absolutely, eternally important is what Jesus explained to His disciples hours before He was crucified. Jesus knew that He would die, rise again, and ascend to Heaven. Because He would no longer be on earth with His disciples, He promised that God the Father would send the Holy Spirit to be with them forever.

I hope that through this study you will grasp the truth of Who the Holy Spirit is. The disciples didn't want Jesus to leave them, but Jesus knew He had to go, so that the Holy Spirit could be sent to all who believe in Him.

I asked my father to share what he teaches from the book of John, and he said he stresses three, simple, key points. It is my delight to quote him word for word below:

> One – belief in Jesus is our passport to Heaven.
>
> Two - the Holy Spirit provides God's power to us for daily living,
>
> And three – we can only do God's will as we allow the Holy Spirit to work through us.
>
> \- George E. Bagwell III

I am so very thankful for all the teaching I have received from my earthly father! And I am eternally thankful to God the Father for giving Jesus as our Savior and the Holy Spirit as our life, counselor, and strength.

My Bible Story

I love my Bible! But I have about 15 of them on my bookshelf, including a Hebrew and a Greek translation, so which one do I love to use for reading and studying? I'd like to answer that question with my Bible story.

The earliest Bible that I remember reading was a children's New Testament Living Bible. It was a birthday present from a friend when I was eight years old! I tried to read the book of Revelation but didn't get very far.

The next Bible that I received was a King James Version from my parents and it was my church Bible. I don't remember reading it, but I must have taken it to Sunday School with me because I found a Psalm 23 bookmark in it. That was the first well-known Scripture to me.

When I was fourteen I began using a Bible which my father felt was an excellent translation. The New English Bible is not very well known, but it was the Bible that made me begin to know God's Word, especially the letter to the Ephesians. I underlined verses and took it to Bible studies in high school.

My first Bible with cross-references and helpful notes was the Ryrie Study Bible in the King James Version. I bought it after high school graduation and used it for my quiet times and Bible study and sermon notes for about 10 years — through college and early marriage and the births of my children! It was falling apart and the bookbinder recommended a durable covering: blue canvas. I call it my blue jean Bible now!

Then I became aware of the New King James Version and decided it would be nice to leave behind Thee's and Thou's of the Old King James… so I bought The Woman's Study Bible NJKV. It was refreshing to read God's truths in a new translation in a Bible that had clean pages on which for me to make new notes. Familiar verses were lovely and overlooked verses began to stand out as they had not before. The changing of Bible translations became a new adventure for me.

I have read through the Bible in the NIV, NLT, NET, NAS, NKJ, ESV, HCSB and The Complete Jewish Bible. It's description states: "Easily see how the Old Testament points to Jesus and quickly get a handle on all major Jewish customs! Enjoy seeing Hebrew keywords. Easily get a handle on the Jewish roots of Christianity!"

I've received precious Bibles as gifts, including a friend's German Bible, my grandmother's 100-year-old-Bible that my mother remembered from her childhood, and one that I call my "coloring Bible" which allows me to meditate on, color and delight in Scriptures which have been illustrated.

Jesus loves me this I know, for my Bible tells me so! I love God's Word and I love my Bible — whichever one I may be reading at any given time.

Do You Know Jesus?

This is the most important question in this study. Please notice that I didn't ask you if you know about Jesus. But do you know Him, personally?

The Bible teaches that God loves you: "For God so loved the world . . . that He gave His one and only son that whoever believes in Him will not perish, but have eternal life." John 3:16 ESV

And it teaches that God wants you to know Him personally: "Now this is eternal life, that men may know Him, the only true God, and Jesus Christ whom He has sent." John 17:3 ESV

But . . . people are separated from God by their sin: "Your sinful acts have alienated you from your God" Isaiah 59:2 NET

Sin causes us to miss the very best for our life: "Jesus said, 'I came that you might have life and have it to the full." John 10:10 NIV

Sin causes us to face death and judgment: "The wages of sin is death." Romans 3:32 NAS "Those who do not know God . . . will pay the penalty of eternal destruction away from the presence of the Lord." 2 Thessalonians 1:8-9 NAS

But there is a solution! Jesus Christ died and conquered death for you! We deserve death and judgment, but Jesus took upon Himself the punishment for our sins, so that we could have a personal relationship with God: "For there is only one God and one Mediator who can reconcile God and humanity-- the man Christ Jesus. He gave his life to purchase freedom for everyone." 1 Timothy 2:5-6 NLT

It's not enough just to know this. Each of us by faith must receive Jesus Christ if we want to know God personally: "To all who have received Him—those who believe in His name—He has given the right to become God's children." John 1:12 NET "For it is by grace you have been saved, through faith—and this not from yourselves, it is the gift of God." Ephesians 2:8 NIV

The ABC's of faith involve:
<u>Acknowledging your need</u>—admitting you have sinned and desiring to turn from sin. (1 John 1:8-9)
<u>Believing Jesus Christ died in your place</u> and rose again to be your Savior—providing forgiveness for your sins. (1 Corinthians 15:3-4:17)
<u>Choosing to invite Christ</u> to direct your life. (Romans 10:9)

Your desire to have a personal relationship with God can be expressed through a simple prayer like this: "Dear Lord, I want to know You personally. Thank you for sending Jesus who died in my place and rose again to be my Savior. Please forgive my sins. I am willing, with your help, to turn from my sins. Come into my life and lead me. Amen."

For illustrations and more information, go to **KnowHimPersonally.com**

Helpful Hints

If you are new to in-depth Bible study: You will need a Bible. Please feel free to use the version of your choice. There are many translations. If you are using a Catholic Bible or a Jewish Old Testament it will be helpful for you to also use a modern version of the Bible which includes the Old and New Testament.

I recommend the following versions which are available for free at online Bible study websites, in smartphone and tablet apps (see recommendations on the next page), or for purchase in Christian bookstores. They are usually referred to by the letters in parentheses.

New King James Version (NKJV)　　New American Standard Version (NASB)
New International Version (NIV)　　Holman Christian Standard Bible (HCSB)
English Standard Version (ESV)　　Legacy Standard Bible (LSB)

This study was written using multiple translations. I have found that I can gain understanding of the meaning of verses by reading other versions of the same passage. Two other popular Bibles are *The Message* and the New Living Translation (NLT); these are both wonderful versions for comparative reading, but are not as appropriate for in-depth study.

Planning time for your lesson. Set aside a specific amount of time to work on the lesson. One lesson may take 30-45 minutes depending on your familiarity with the Scriptures. You may want to do the lessons in shorter increments of time, depending on your schedule and personal preferences. I find that I absorb, retain, and apply the message of the Scriptures better when I am not rushed.

Please begin your study time with prayer. Ask the Holy Spirit to give you understanding of God's Word, as it is promised that He will do according to 1 Corinthians 2:12-13: "Now we have received, not the spirit of the world, but the Spirit who is from God, that we might know the things freely given to us by God, which things we also speak, not in words taught by human wisdom, but in those taught by the Spirit, combining spiritual thoughts with spiritual words." I have given you a reminder at the beginning of each lesson.

Observation, interpretation, and application. The Scripture readings, activities, cross-references and word definitions are all placed in the order which is most appropriate to your study. It is best to follow this order if you can, rather than skipping steps or setting steps aside to be completed at a different time. The order follows the inductive study process: observation (what the Scripture says), interpretation (what the author intended, what the Scripture means) and application (what difference the Scripture makes in your life). You will be doing the research, cross-referencing and summarization of the truths of each passage. When you finish a study of a passage, you will have gleaned more understanding on your own than you will find in some commentaries!

Looking up Hebrew word definitions. One of the activities included to help you understand the correct interpretation of the scripture is discovering and considering the definition of a word in its original language. Please make sure that you look up the definition of the word in its original language, not the definition of the English word. You will be given a prompt like this:

> **Abide: Strong's #3306**
> **Greek word:**
> **Greek definition:**

There are several ways you can look up the words given.

- You can google the Strong's reference number (Strong's 3306) and your web browser will give you links to the definition.
- You can go to an online Bible study website (recommendations below) and use their free reference materials. Look for study tabs, lexicons (this is what Hebrew and Greek word dictionaries are called), concordances and original language tools. There are search boxes where you can type in the Strong's reference number. Use G before the number for Greek words (G3306).

> biblehub.com   studylight.org   biblehub.com

Suggested resources, described on page 94, are also available at these websites if you want to do more research on your own.

- You can download free Bible study apps such as **Literal Word** and **BibleHub** for your smartphone and/or tablet. I use **MySword** which allows me to go to a passage and click on the Strong's reference number next to the word. Try a few different ones and see what you like best.
- You may have some great resources on your own bookshelves! Enjoy using books like: *Strong's Exhaustive Concordance* and *The Complete Word Study Dictionary* by Spiros Zhodiates.

If you have trouble, it would be better to skip the exercise rather than filling in the English definition.

It's about your head and your heart. My hope is that you will read portions of Scripture and gain understanding of what is being communicated through them so that you can consider how to apply the truth of God's Word to your life. I have tried to make the study "user-friendly" and I promise that I don't ask trick questions. I do want to make you think hard sometimes though! I hope you won't get overwhelmed. Do what you can, a little bit at a time. The reward of knowing our holy God through His recorded word far outweighs the time and effort of study.

Prayer requests and praises. You will find pages at the end of this workbook which provide prompts from Scriptures for your prayers as well as a place for you to write out a personal prayer request . If you are studying with a group, it would be helpful to reflect on your personal prayer request before sharing it with the group. Keep your requests brief and personal. This page is also a place to record the prayer requests of others.

LESSON 1

A View from Above

JOHN'S GOSPEL

"Abide in Me," Jesus said; "I am the vine, you are the branches. He who abides in Me, and I in him, bears much fruit; for without Me you can do nothing." John 15:5

This statement from Jesus means so much to me. It means so much to all of us. It's an illustration of our intimate relationship with Jesus which is made possible by the indwelling Holy Spirit. We will learn more about this throughout this study.

Because of the precious truths of this verse, images of vineyards and grapevines laden with bunches of fruit are enjoyed by many, including me! But there is another aspect to the truth of John 15:5, and something critical to note regarding vineyards. All the work is done by the vinedresser and the vine. And that's a lot of work.

The vine must be planted in good soil, in a good climate, and be tended year round. Branches must be trained as to which way to grow and they must be pruned wisely. The vine may have to endure severe heat, dangerous drought, and freezing winters.

When we see a beautiful, well-kept vineyard that produces a bountiful harvest, it's the result of years of toil by the vineyard keeper. The lovely, refreshing, cheerful vineyard is the result of hard work, perseverance, and overcoming many difficulties.

This is an excellent illustration of what God the Father and our Savior Jesus did for us. The Father is the vinedresser who watches over and cares for the vineyard, the vine and the branches; Jesus is the Vine who endured all the harsh conditions and came forth with an abundant harvest.

Jesus used the illustration of the vine and the branches as He communicated His last, intimate, comforting message to His disciples before His death. You will see that it is the centerpiece, the focal point, of John 13:31-16:33. The illustration of the vine and the branches summarizes what He taught them. To put it another way, everything Jesus said in John 14 and John 16 was illustrated through the vine and the branches imagery. I hope you'll be able to see this as we study the whole message.

Before we go to the vineyard of John 15, let's get a view from above to take in the landscape in which the vineyard is found. We need an overview of the book of John and an overview of Jesus' life. We need to see what was happening when Jesus said "abide in Me." That's what our first lesson will give us. The rest of the study will be a close examination of and meditation on the truths that Jesus shared with His disciples less than 24 hours before He died.

In the Greek, this book is simply called "According to John." Nowhere does John identify himself by name, but refers to himself as "the beloved disciple." He writes from a personal encounter and intimate relationship with Jesus. He knew Jesus. He walked and talked and lived with Him. John testifies of the One whom he saw and heard and loved.

It is going to be a special treat to hear from the one who knew Jesus so well and stayed close to Him even through His death.

John gives a clear introduction and conclusion that leave no doubt as to the reason for his writing. The first 18 verses of his book summarize everything that John will tell us about Jesus, His life, and His message.

Please read John 1:1-18.

What words or phrases indicate that Jesus is eternal?

What words or phrases indicate that Jesus is One with God (which means that Jesus Himself is God)?

What names and statements in this passage describe Jesus?

The beloved disciple introduces Jesus. The descriptions in this passage show that Jesus is more than a man; they show us that He is God. And yet He is God Who became flesh and dwelt among us! His coming had an impact on the entire world. Some rejected Him, but others received Him and believed in Him.

John 1:1-18 introduces concepts that will show up throughout the whole gospel of John. Jesus gives life. Jesus is the light. Jesus is full of grace. Jesus is full of truth. Jesus shows the glory of God.

In chapters 1–12, John wrote of Jesus' public ministry and recorded seven signs that Jesus performed. Some refer to John 1–12 as the book of signs. They were given as evidence of Jesus' identity. Let's take a brief look at these amazing signs. We also call them miracles!

List the big events in the following passages that show that Jesus was not just an ordinary man. He had the power to do the miraculous.

1st Sign: John 2:1-11 _____

2nd Sign: John 4:46-54 _____

3rd Sign: John 5:1-9 _____

4th Sign: John 6:1-11 _____

5th Sign: John 6:16-21 _____

6th Sign: John 9:1-11 _____

7th Sign: John 11:38-44 _____

In each of these passages, John gave enough detail to show that the miracles were no small coincidences. Each situation presented a hopeless scenario. But Jesus – with a word or without, with a touch or without – overcame each dilemma and disease and even death. Nothing was too difficult for Him.

What else did John write about so that we would believe that Jesus is the Son of God, the Messiah? He tells us more in the second half of his book.

Chapters 13–20 are sometimes referred to as the book of glory. John recorded the private discussions that Jesus had with His disciples where He revealed Himself to them and prepared them for their mission after His death and resurrection. We will be studying John 13:31-16:33 which contains the last message that Jesus gave His disciples before His death.

To get a bird's eye view of the book of the glory of Jesus, complete the following statements:

In John 13:1-7, Jesus shows Himself as the Servant of the Lord when He
_____.

In John 14:6, Jesus shows Himself as the _____ as He promises to go and prepare a place for all of His disciples to be together.

In John 15:1-5, Jesus describes Himself as _____, in whom we are to abide.

In John 16:7, Jesus explains that He is going away but will send the Holy Spirit as our _____.

In John 17:5-9, Jesus reveals Himself as the Son who has submitted to and glorified the Father as He _____ for his disciples and all those who will believe.

The final chapters of John 18-21 show the glory of Jesus as He laid down His life for us, then was resurrected and appeared to Mary and the disciples.

Let's enjoy that amazing moment of weeping turned to joy!

What happened according to John 20:15-20?

We looked at John's introduction to his book and his declaration of Who Jesus is. We noted the signs and the glory of Jesus. What was John's conclusion to his writing?

What was his goal according to John 20:31?

John praised Jesus from the beginning of his book to the very end. He began in John 1:16 with "from the fullness of His grace we have all received one blessing after another;" and recorded Peter's words in John 6:68-69^{NKJ}: "Lord, to whom shall we go? You have the words of eternal life. Also we have come to believe and know that You are the Christ, the Son of the living God."

John finished with a statement of awe and wonder at the life of Jesus saying in John 21:25: "And there are also many other things that Jesus did, which if they were written one by one, I suppose that even the world itself could not contain the books that would be written."

Jesus did and said so many wonderful things! The gospels include every teaching we need to hear.

How well do we know what has been recorded?

What are some of Jesus' messages and miracles which are most familiar to you?

I look forward to focusing on John 13:31-16:33, the extremely important, heart-to-heart, final message from Jesus to His disciples before His death.

What is your favorite thing about Jesus from today's lesson?

LESSON 2

An Exclusive Meeting

JOHN 13:31-16:33

Soon, Jesus will tell His disciples that He is sending the Holy Spirit as the Helper. We need His help no matter what we are doing! You'll see a prompt to pause and pray at the beginning of each lesson.

Please pray that the Holy Spirit will help you now as you begin to consider Jesus' message.

In the previous lesson, we noted that Jesus showed Himself as the Servant of the Lord by washing the feet of the disciples. This event occurred at the beginning of what we now call the Last Supper. Jesus and all 12 of His disciples were celebrating the Passover meal together.

It was at this meal that Jesus started sharing His very important last words of promises, plans, and purposes. But His message was not for all 12 disciples.

What did Jesus declare in John 13:21?

How did the disciples respond, according to John 13:22-25?

Jesus answered, "It is the one to whom I will give this piece of bread when I have dipped it in the dish." **John 13:26** NIV

That seems clear, doesn't it? But it wasn't. All the disciples had been sharing the Passover meal with Jesus. Dipping bread into bitter herbs was a regular part of the meal and happened several times.

Only John knew of Jesus' answer, but even he didn't understand what was happening at that moment. Jesus had not given an indication of the timing of His betrayal and all the disciples were asking: "Lord, is it I?"

What happened next, according to John 13:27-30?

We know the rest of the story now. Things became clear to the eleven disciples later, but at the dinner they remained perplexed even though the traitor left the meal.

While Judas is definitely the traitor and a villain, behind the scenes the most evil villain of all is Satan. He is named in this passage for the first and only time in John's gospel. The fallen angel and enemy of God is always at war against Him and His people.

> **"Now it was night"** (John 13:30) is a parenthetical note by the author. The comment is more than just a time indicator, however. With the departure of Judas to set in motion the betrayal, arrest, trials, crucifixion, and death of Jesus, daytime is over and night has come (see John 9:5; 11:9–10; 12:35–36). Judas had become one of those who walked by night and stumbled, because the light was not in him (11:10).[1]

What did Jesus declare and promise in John 8:12?

Do you have the light of life? If you answered yes, can others see it in your life? If you answered no, or if you're not sure, please turn to page 11 entitled "Do You Know Jesus?" and consider what is explained there.

Now we have the setting and the context for Jesus' last message. He knew that Judas was about to lead soldiers and temple guards to arrest Him. Jesus only had a few more hours alone with His eleven disciples. He had important instructions and comforting promises for them.

With this in mind, please read the first portion of Jesus' message that was given while the disciples were still gathered in the upper room. I've outlined it below, based on the statements of Jesus and the questions of the disciples.

Make brief notes about Jesus' statements, and record each disciple's name (if given) and his response. We're continuing our view from above so that we can see Jesus' whole message.

Jesus' 1st statement: John 13:31-35

1st response: John 13:36-38

Jesus' 2nd statement: John 14:1-4

2nd response: John 14:5

Jesus' 3rd statement: John 14:6-7

3rd response: John 14:8

Jesus' 4th statement: John 14:9-21

4th response: John 14:22

Jesus' 5th statement: John 14:23-31

> The specific issue that the lengthy discourse addresses is the fact that Jesus is about to return to the Father and hence will no longer be physically present with the disciples. They will continue to follow Him, however, and wait for His future return. It is this time of waiting and watching that Jesus specifically has in mind throughout the discourse. What are the disciples to do? And, how are they to carry on His work until He returns? [2]

We are now in the period of time that Jesus was referring to, the time that He is with the Father in Heaven, and we are still on earth. What in His message so far is comforting to you?

The next section of Jesus' message contains one of my favorite portions of Scripture and one of my favorite words found in the Bible. Let's continue reading what Jesus shared with His disciples.

Please read John 15:1-16:16.

Make brief notes of words or phrases that are meaningful to you or about which you have questions.

Based on John 16:17-18, summarize the disciples' response to what Jesus said.

Jesus responded to their confusion with a further explanation.

Please read John 16:19-28.

What is the main point of John 16:20-24?

How did the disciples respond to Jesus' statements in John 16:25-28? (See John 16:29-30.)

Please read Jesus' concluding exhortation to His friends, found in John 16:31-33.

What was the sober warning to them?

What did Jesus want them to have?

What did Jesus declare would be the outcome of laying down His life?

This has been an overview of this precious message of Jesus found only in John's gospel. I am so thankful that the beloved disciple listened closely to Jesus and the Holy Spirit reminded him of what He said, so that we too could be instructed and encouraged and given the great hope of these promises.

There are many topics and meaningful words in these chapters. Conclude this lesson by choosing one thing that stands out to you the most right now.

LESSON 3

The Plan

JOHN 13:31-38

I've just had a few days of being in the same house with my little grandsons. It was busy and fun! When they left, even though I knew I would see them again very soon, it still was a very heartfelt moment. I never like to say goodbye to my family! Goodbyes are meaningful and hard, even when you know you'll see your loved ones again. Jesus knew He was saying an extended goodbye to His disciples even though they didn't quite understand it yet.

Please pray that the Holy Spirit will show you the glory of Jesus as you study today.

Please read John 13:31-35.

Fill in the blanks below according to the verses given, based on the NKJV translation. I've given you a blank for each word needed. This exercise is to help you notice repeated words.

So, when Judas had gone out, Jesus said,

John 13:31: _____ the Son of Man _____ _____,

and God _____ _____ in _____.

John 13:32: _____ God _____ _____ in _____,

God will also _____ _____ in Himself,

and _____ Him _____.

John 13:33: Little children, I shall be with you a _____ _____ _____. You will seek Me; and as I said to the Jews, "Where _____ _____ _____, you _____ _____ ," so now I say to you.

John 13:34: A _____ commandment I give to you, that you _____ _____ _____; as I _____ _____ _____, that you also _____ one another.

John 13:35: By this all will know that you are My disciples, if you have _____ for _____ _____.

The repeated words are very clear now, aren't they? But some things might still be confusing.

First, let's notice the timing that Jesus emphasized. Now that Jesus has urged Judas to go quickly and do what he is going to do… Now that Judas has left the room… Now that the betrayal is being carried out… Now that Jesus knows God will glorify Him immediately… Jesus knows the time has come for Him to obey His Father by laying down His life on behalf of sinners.

The gravity of the moment was upon them all, and even though the disciples still didn't understand the full impact of Jesus' death, they did understand that He was talking about dying.

What does Hebrews 2:9 say that Jesus' death brought about for Him?

It will help us understand Jesus' statement in John 13:31-32 by inserting the phrase "by His death." We should also note that "if" means "since" in this sentence based on the Greek construction. I know this will be an awkward repetitive sentence, but let's consider it:

NKJ John 13:31-32: "Now, the Son of man is glorified *by His death,* and *by Jesus' death* God is glorified in Him. *Since by His death* God is glorified by Him, God will also glorify Him *by His death* in Himself and will glorify Him *by His death* immediately!"

"Glorify" means to "magnify the reputation of" and that is certainly what Jesus' death did.[3] There is no one who ever did, or ever could do, what Jesus did in His life, in His death, and in His resurrection.

How did Peter explain it later in his letter, according to 1 Peter 2:22-24?

Jesus knew that His death would occur within the next 24 hours. He only had a little while longer with the disciples.

What was the first thing He told them, according to John 13:34-35?

Was this really a new commandment? Yes, it was! The Israelites knew they were to love the Lord their God, and love their neighbor as themselves. But it was an entirely new thing to love each other as Jesus loved them.

How did Paul describe the love of Jesus in Ephesians 5:2?

What did John say about Jesus in Revelation 1:5-6?

Peter and John heard what Jesus said, then they saw what Jesus suffered on the cross. Later, empowered by the Holy Spirit, they obeyed Jesus, loved as He loved, and glorified Him in their lives.

How does your life magnify the reputation of Jesus?

How can you love your brothers and sisters in the family of God the way Jesus loved?

Peter was listening and had a question. He was eager to follow Jesus and was shocked with Jesus' reply. He had the best intentions. He was a leader among the disciples. But he was about to make wrong choices.

What did Jesus say to Peter in John 13:38?

You can see the full account of Peter's denial in Matthew 26:69-75, Mark 14:66-72, Luke 22:54-62, and John 18:15-27. Because the focus of this study is on Jesus' words, we will only briefly consider Peter's denial.

Pastor James Montgomery Boice notes that there were several steps to Peter's fall into denial of Jesus. First, he was overconfident (John 13:37). Second, he failed to pray (Matthew 26:40-41). Third, he followed at a distance (Luke 22:54). Finally, he put himself amid Jesus' enemies and even benefited from them (Luke 22:55).[4]

Look at the steps of Peter's fall in the commentary above. List appropriate actions you can take through which God will make a way for you to escape temptations.

After His resurrection, Jesus gave Peter the opportunity for restoration and a recommissioning. Three questions. Three replies. Three instructions (John 21:14-22). Peter's denial was forgiven and his passion for following the Lord had a purpose.

LESSON 4

Trust Me

JOHN 14:1-6

We are about to study what may be a familiar passage of Scripture to you. These verses are often read at funerals; John 14:6 was read at my mother's memorial service. This is appropriate because these words of Jesus are intended to comfort His disciples regarding His death and their deaths. Peter may have been asking about life after death when he said to Jesus: "Where are you going?"

The disciples had left their boats and businesses behind to follow Jesus. And now He was going somewhere that they couldn't go? This didn't make sense to them. They had just been told that one of them would betray Jesus and they had just heard that Peter would deny Him.

They were distressed. Confused. To say they were upset is putting it mildly. We can almost sense the tension in the room by noticing how several of the disciples interrupted Jesus' message with questions. Almost like reporters at a press conference trying to get all the details of the event. The disciples were alarmed.

Please pray that the Holy Spirit will open the eyes of your understanding to see God's blessings in His word.

Read John 14:1-6.

What did Jesus say to them in John 14:1 that indicates He knew what they were thinking and feeling?

Troubled is the Greek word **parassestho** and literally means shaken or stirred up. It can be used to indicate acute mental or spiritual agitation, extreme anxiety, and sometimes even a sense of intimidation.

How would you have said it? Jesus' words are so beautiful, even as they address the problem. My paraphrase would be: "Don't be stressed out about what I'm telling you."

What is the solution to their distress, according to John 14:1?

All three verbs in John 14:1 are in the imperative. They are commands. And they belong together. "Let not your heart be troubled" is just an empty statement if it isn't combined with "believe in God, believe also in Me."

*Most translations say **believe**, but the NIV and NLT say **trust**. Both words are a translation of **pisteuo**. But what do you say when you are urging a friend to do something that they're afraid of doing? What do you call the team building exercise when a person falls backward into another's arms? It's a trust fall. And you say, "trust me."*

Do you actively trust Jesus when you are faced with challenging, stressful, confusing circumstances? How do you show that you trust Him? What do you do, or not do?

What did Jesus say in John 14:2-4 to assure His disciples that His death was necessary, and He was trustworthy?

Please look up the following Greek words. Helpful hints for this exercise are on page 13.

Mansions: Strong's # 3438

Greek word:

Greek definition:

Root word of mansions: Strong's #3306

Greek word:

Greek definition:

*Did those words and definitions surprise you? The term **mansion** is not the best translation of the Greek word. It comes from the Latin **mansiones.** Jesus wasn't talking about lifestyles of the rich and famous. He was talking about something far better.*

"My Father's house," which Jesus used to refer to the temple in John 2:16, ultimately refers to the presence of God.

> Rooms [mone] in such a house signifies nothing less than the sheer delight of forever dwelling in the unshielded radiance of the glory of God.[5]

Let's look ahead at what Jesus says as He explains things further.

Where is Jesus going, based on John 14:2 and John 14:12?

How did Jesus go there, according to Luke 23:33 and Luke 23:42-46?

> God's domain has plenty of room, and the preparation of Jesus for our entrance into that domain was through His "departure" or death on the cross. The Gospel of John is not trying to portray Jesus as being in the construction business of building or renovating rooms. Rather, Jesus was in the business of leading people to God.[6]

Jesus was making the way for us to get to His Father's house! I look forward to being there with Him!

What does Hebrews 6:19-20 tell us about what Jesus has done and where He is now?

What did Jesus do for us and where can we go now, according to Hebrews 10:19-20?

Later in his life, John was given a revelation of things to come. He must have enjoyed the sneak peek of the Father's house.

What did John see in Revelation 21:2-3? How was it described?

What did John see in Revelation 22:1-6?

Let's review the very comforting declarations Jesus gave to His troubled disciples.

Read John 14:1-6.

What are we waiting for based on John 14:3?

What is indisputable, based on John 14:6?

Peter came to understand and proclaim this truth. What did he say about Jesus and the way to the Father's house, according to Acts 4:8-12?

There's a hymn that's been floating around in my thoughts as I've contemplated Jesus' tender and reassuring words. Based on my study, I've changed the lyrics just a little bit, which I've underlined on the next page. But I'm thankful for the insights and creativity of the author Eliza E. Hewitt, poet and Sunday school teacher, and composer Emily D. Wilson who entitled the tune "Heaven." [7] *Those who know Jesus as the way to the Father's house have been rejoicing through this hymn since 1898.*

When We All Get To Heaven

Words by Eliza E. Hewitt **Music by Emily D. Wilson**

Sing the wondrous love of Jesus,
Sing His mercy and His grace;
In the mansions bright and blessed
<u>He has prepared</u> for us a place.

Chorus:
When we all get to heaven,
What a day of rejoicing that will be!
When we all see Jesus,
We'll sing and shout the victory.

While we walk the pilgrim pathway
Clouds will overspread the sky;
But when trav'ling days are over,
Not a shadow, not a sigh.

Chorus

Let us then be true and faithful,
Trusting, serving ev'ry day;
Just one glimpse of Him in glory
Will the toils of life repay.

Chorus

Onward to the prize before us!
Soon His beauty we'll behold;
Soon the pearly gates will open;
We shall tread the streets of gold.

LESSON 5

The Need to Know

JOHN 14:6-14

They are listening intently. One answer from Jesus leads to another question from the disciples. Praise the Lord for His patience with us! We are very often, as the disciples were, slow learners. The depth of theology communicated by Jesus was overwhelming then and still is today. The truth of our triune God is the foundation of Jesus' farewell message.

First we will consider the relationship between God the Father and God the Son.

Please pray that the Holy Spirit will teach you the deep things of God.

Please read John 14:6-11.

Who do we need to know so that we will know God the Father?

How does Jesus describe His relationship with God the Father, according to John 14:10-11?

The disciples wanted to know and needed to know but didn't know the full significance of who Jesus is. They knew His name, His family, His wisdom, and His obedience to God's word. But they had not connected the dots that Jesus was God in the flesh. I'm not holding that against them. The whole world changed when God was born in the manger!

Matthew the disciple came to understand this later. How did he explain that Jesus the man was God in the flesh, in Matthew 1:20-23?

Jesus said: "From now on you know Him (the Father) and have seen Him." Philip didn't understand the connection, so he said, "Lord, show us the Father, and we will be satisfied." John 14:7 NLT

Many commentators think that Philip was asking for a theophany of God – a physical, visible manifestation of God. And to his credit, Philip believed that Jesus could answer the request.

How did Jesus respond to Philip, according to John 14:9?

To put it as simply as our little minds can fathom: To see Jesus is to see the Father. As simple as that is, it is still hard to comprehend. It is profound.

What two evidences did Jesus point to that show that seeing Jesus is seeing the Father, according to John 14:10-11?

> Through His sinless, perfect humanity the disciples could see deity. They could see the Father in action in the Son. They could know what the Father was like because they knew what Jesus was like. They could hear the Father in everything Jesus said. They could see the Father in everything Jesus did. They could know the Father because they knew the Son. What Jesus was, God was. He was in the Father; the Father was in Him.[8]

How do the following verses explain that seeing Jesus is seeing God?

2 Corinthians 4:6

Colossians 1:15

Hebrews 1:1-3

What **works** had the disciples seen Jesus do that testified to His deity? A few examples are given below. Briefly note what you learn.

Matthew 14:24-33

Matthew 15:30-31

Mark 6:41-44

Luke 4:33-36

What other miracles of Jesus come to mind that testify of His deity?

What **words** did Jesus speak that testified to His deity? Briefly note them from the examples given below.

Matthew 7:21-23

Mark 2:5-7

Luke 10:17-19

John 8:56-59

You know there are many more words and works recorded in the gospels. And we've already noted that John supposed that all the books in the world couldn't contain everything Jesus said and did (John 21:25).

Jesus said: "Believe Me that I am in the Father and the Father in Me."

Please describe what you believe about Jesus.

What is the incredible consequence of knowing the full significance of who Jesus is? Record Jesus' promise from John 14:12-14.

Jesus did amazing things and yet He said that we would do even greater things. This has always surprised me. There are two ways to look at the word "greater" and both are appropriate. Jesus ministered for three years in Israel and His disciples have been ministering for over 2000 years around the world. A greater number of works have been done in that time than could be done in three years.

It is also appropriate to say that greater works have been done through disciples of Jesus since the giving of the Holy Spirit at Pentecost. Jesus healed the eyes of the blind, but preaching the gospel opens the eyes of the spiritually blind. Jesus raised the dead, but proclaiming the truth of His resurrection allows those dead in sins to be born again to new life.

Jesus made a promise about prayer as well. While we can ask for anything, there are boundaries given. Asking in Jesus' name means that we are asking for what is in accordance with His character and it means that we are asking based on our faith in who He is. Remember, He is God in the flesh. We should also consider prayer in coordination with His next statement.

Write out John 14:14-15.

How can loving Jesus and keeping His commandments influence our prayers?

Prayer is a precious part of our relationship with God. Jesus has more to tell us about it later in His message.

LESSON 6

It's All About Love

JOHN 14:15-26

Love. Love. Love. That's what it's all about! Yes, it is! There are many things to cover in the passage we will study. And they are all related to loving Jesus for Who He is and what He did.

――― ――― ―――

Pray that the Holy Spirit will assure you of His presence as you study today.

――― ――― ―――

Jesus said something to His eleven disciples that they hadn't heard before. We're very used to it, but just think about those men hearing it for the first time.

What did Jesus say in John 14:15?

Put yourself in the disciples' sandals. They've just been told Jesus is going away and they are distressed. Now He says they are to love Him and keep His commandments. What do you think their response might have been?

Might they have thought – Jesus has taught us a lot. How do we remember everything He commanded? How do we do everything He commanded? The Pharisees won't be very happy with us. And Jesus has been keeping our prideful egos in check, who's going to do it now?

Of course, Jesus knew the problem the disciples would have. He and the Father had a plan.

Please read John 14:15-26.

List the details about the Holy Spirit according to the following verses:

John 14:16

John 14:17

John 14:26

These verses have the obvious statements about the Holy Spirit. But Jesus did explain more about His presence in this passage.

What do the following phrases indicate about the relationship between Jesus and the Holy Spirit? John 14:19 – "I will come to you;" John 14:20 – "and I in you;" John 14:23 – "We will come to him and make our home with him."

These statements echo the promises of the New Covenant. What did the Lord say through Jeremiah 31:31-34 and Ezekiel 36:26-27?

Keep in mind that Jesus' death, resurrection, and ascension were just about to take place. Why did Jesus say that He would send the Holy Spirit, according to John 14:18?

John used a special word for the Holy Spirit that doesn't have an adequate equivalent in the English language and only he used it.

Please look up the definition for the following words:

Counselor: Strong's #3875

Greek word:

Greek definition:

Please read John 14:15-26 again.

What did Jesus say about the world in the following verses?

John 14:17

John 14:19

What did Judas ask in John 14:22? Write out his question.

Judas (not Iscariot – not the traitor) heard Jesus' announcement and something didn't make sense to him. To his credit, he called Jesus "Lord." To his credit, he was comprehending that something big was about to happen. But he, like the rest of the disciples, was eager to see Jesus reveal His position as Messiah, free Israel from Roman rule, and take His seat on the throne of the kingdom.

They had heard prophecies straight from Jesus' own mouth:

At that time the sign of the Son of Man will appear in the sky, and all the nations of the earth will mourn. They will see the Son of Man coming on the clouds of the sky, with power and great glory. **Matthew 24:30** NIV

Perhaps the phrase Jesus used in John 14:20, "at that day," triggered in Judas thoughts of Old Testament prophecies of what would happen in the future "at that day."

According to John 14:23-24, what did Jesus emphasize in His response to Judas? And what did He indicate about the world?

Throughout this portion of Jesus' message, He repeated that we are to love Him and keep His word. While Jesus gave many lessons and instructions during His life, He regularly urged all to "repent, for the kingdom of heaven is near" (Matthew 4:17).

The Pharisees and Sadducees, the Jews, the Greeks, and all the world around Him did not respond appropriately. They rejected Jesus rather than receiving Him as the One sent from God.

Please read John 14:15-26 again.

Jesus referred to **His death** and **His resurrection** in this passage. Note which one He is referring to in the following phrases:

John 14:18 – "leave you" – _____

John 14:19 – "A little while longer and the world will see me no more" – _____

John 14:19 – "but you will see Me" – _____

John 14:19 – "Because I live" – _____

John 14:25 – "These things I have spoken while being present with you" – _____

Every word out of Jesus' mouth is important, isn't it?! There's one more point to look at now.

Fill in the blanks according to John 14:19-20 (NKJV). "A little while longer and the world will see Me no more, but you will see Me. Because I live, you _____ _____ _____. At that day you will know that I am in My Father, and _____ _____ _____ , and _____ _____ _____.

These are words of eternal life! His life and our lives as well. His death was not the end. Have you ever realized that Jesus never said to His disciples: "I'm about to die"? He described His death, as we saw in John 13:31, as the time when He would be glorified. It was terrible and wonderful at the same time.

Let's see how Paul described what Jesus was talking about in John 14:19-20.

What does Romans 8:9-10 say?

*Before His death, Jesus promised that He would send the Holy Spirit to the disciples. This would be a brand new situation for them and for all who believe in Jesus' message. The promise was fulfilled 50 days after Jesus' resurrection, at the Jewish festival called Feast of Weeks. We refer to it as Pentecost, based on the Greek word **pentekoste** which means fiftieth. The giving of the Holy Spirit is described in Acts 2:1-47.*

Look again at John 14:20 and Romans 8:9-10. Fill in the blanks below based on these two references, using either: **the Spirit** or **Christ.**

_____ is in you.

_____ is in you.

You are in _____.

You are in _____.

I want to repeat, and emphasize, that these are words of eternal life! If you don't have the Holy Spirit in you, then you don't have eternal life. If you do have the Spirit in you, you have life. This can also be stated as having life in Christ.

The phrase "in Christ" is so very important that we need to spend time considering what it means.

Note the blessings that we have **in Christ** from the verses below:

Romans 6:11

1 Corinthians 1:2

2 Corinthians 5:17

Ephesians 1:3

Colossians 3:3

1 Peter 5:14

*Jesus said: "On that day, you will know that I am in the Father, and you in Me, and I in you" (John 14:20). He declared a spiritual truth that could not happen until the Holy Spirit was given. But now, **in Christ**, because of the indwelling and enlightening Holy Spirit, we experience this intimate union.*

Read the commentary below and highlight phrases that are meaningful to you.

> One of the most precious truths in all Scripture is the doctrine of the believer's union with the Lord Jesus Christ. The concept of being united to Christ speaks of the most vital spiritual intimacy that one can imagine between the Lord and His people. While Christ relates to believers as Lord, Master, Savior, and Teacher, they are not merely associated with Christ as the object of His saving grace and love. It is not that Christians merely worship Jesus, obey Him or pray to Him, thought surely those privileges would be enough. Rather, they are so intimately identified with Him and He with them that Scripture says that they are united. He is in them and they are in Him.
>
> Most commonly represented by the tiny preposition "in," the believer's union with Christ permeates the New Testament. Believers are often said to be "in Christ" (1 Cor. 1:30; 2 Cor. 5:17), "in the Lord" (Rom. 16:11), and "in Him" (1 John 5:20). Similarly, Christ is also said to be in His people (Rom. 8:10; 2 Cor. 13:5; Eph. 3:17), a notion that Paul defines as the very "hope of glory" itself (Col. 1:27). Sometimes both of these aspects of union with Christ are presented in the same text, only further emphasizing the intimacy of the mutual indwelling of Christ and the believer (e.g. John 6:56; 15:4; 1 John 4:13). Clearly, the importance of the believer's union with Christ cannot be overstated.[9]

To conclude this lesson, review what the Holy Spirit does in our lives and what it means to be in Christ. Are you enjoying the gift of the Spirit and life in Christ?

LESSON 7

His Gift of Peace

JOHN 14:27-31

Peace and joy. Peace? And joy? In these moments before Jesus' death? This is exactly what Jesus brought to their attention. Peace and joy would be the results of His death.

――― ――― ―――

Ask the Holy Spirit to strengthen your faith and give you courage.

――― ――― ―――

Please read John 14:27-31.

Jesus repeats several things in this passage. The disciples needed to hear them more than once.

What does He repeat in John 14:27-28, either in the same sentence or from a previous statement?

Peace in the Hebrew is **shalom** *and is used as a greeting and a goodbye. But that isn't how Jesus is using it now. He says it is His gift to His disciples. He is giving much more than a word of calmness and serenity.*

What does Romans 5:1 say?

According to Ephesians 2:13-18, what was the problem and what did Jesus do?

The peace that Jesus gives through His departure (His death) is peace with God.

> "This peace," says Jesus, "is both a legacy which I leave behind and a treasure which I give." Peace in John 14:27, in light of the whole chapter, indicates that absence of spiritual unrest and that assurance of salvation and of God's loving presence under all circumstance, which results from exercising faith in God and in His Son and from the contemplation of His gracious promises.[10]

Jesus repeated "let not your heart be troubled." He knew that His going away would bring about life-changing blessings. At this point, He stated "don't be afraid." Why shouldn't they be afraid? How could they not be afraid?

What did Jesus say in John 14:1? Let not your heart be troubled. _____.

What did Jesus say in John 14:27? Let not your heart be troubled, _____.

Write out the following verses:

Psalm 56:3

Psalm 56:11

Isaiah 12:2

Why should we not be afraid according to Psalm 23:4?

Jesus was about to depart, but He promised He would be with us in the person of the Holy Spirit.

According to John 14:28, why were the disciples to rejoice?

Can you imagine the look on their faces when He said this? They didn't understand then, but the Holy Spirit did remind them and enlighten them regarding all that Jesus said.

Paul tells us to rejoice with those who rejoice (Romans 12:15). Jesus certainly rejoiced when He finished His work on the cross and returned to His Father in glory. His departure from earth meant that He was going home.

> In their thoughts and meditations, the disciples had been concentrating too much on themselves. Had they loved Jesus sufficiently, they would have realized that this departure would bring glory to Him! Seeing this, they would have rejoiced.[11]

Have you noticed the phrase, "the Father is greater than I"? Some, like Unitarians, Jehovah's Witnesses, and other cults misuse this statement to teach that Jesus is not God. We have already seen that Jesus clearly teaches that He and God the Father are One. His statement that the Father is greater is in reference to Jesus' incarnation – being made a man. Other passages of Scripture will help us see this further.

What does Philippians 2:5-11 tell us about Jesus' deity and His humanity?

What does Hebrews 2:9 tell us about Jesus' humanity?

In the beginning was the Word, and the Word was with God, and the Word was God. And the Word became flesh and dwelt among us, and we beheld His glory, the glory as of the only begotten of the Father, full of grace and truth. **John 1:1, 14** NKJ

Jesus was with God in the beginning. He was God. And then became flesh. He had a mission to accomplish.

How many times did Jesus tell His disciples that He was going to die? At least three times before this message at the Passover meal, and then as we have seen, He has repeatedly referred to His death as His departure.

Note the details Jesus predicted regarding His death from the verses below:

Matthew 16:21

Matthew 17:22-23

Matthew 20:17-19

And now I have told you before it comes, that when it does come to pass, you may believe. **John 14:29** NKJ

> When they see these things happen, their level of trust in Jesus will increase and their concept of who He is will expand. The confession of Thomas in John 20:28 is representative of this increased understanding of who Jesus is.[12]

According to John 14:30, how does Jesus indicate that His death is about to occur?

> The prince of this world is the devil (John 12:31; 16:11). Since it says he is coming, Jesus is undoubtedly referring to the activity of the devil in moving Judas to betray him to his enemies, which he was probably doing at that very moment (13:27, 30). In the person of Judas, Satan was literally coming to initiate Christ's arrest and crucifixion.[13]

Satan was coming, but he had no power, no claim, no hold on Jesus. There was no sin in Jesus and Satan had no authority over Him.

How did Jesus express His voluntary obedience to His Father in John 14:31?

The ruler of the world was about to do his evil worst and show his hate, but the Creator of the world was about to show the world the power of His love.

LESSON 8

The Vinedresser and The Vineyard

JOHN 15:1-6

As we begin to study John 15:1-6, picture the winter season when much attention is given to the vineyard. We need to walk with the vinedresser and see how he takes care of his vines and branches.

Jesus uses an extended metaphor to illustrate His teaching about His presence with the disciples through the indwelling Holy Spirit. This illustration is the focal point of His entire message recorded in John 13:31-16:33. Some think that He was leading His disciples through a vineyard outside the city while on their way to the garden where He would soon be arrested.

Pray that the Holy Spirit will encourage you through the words of Jesus.

Please read John 15:1-6.

In John 15:1, 5, Jesus calls Himself: _____

In John 15:1, He calls the Father: _____

In John 15:5, He calls His disciples: _____

Jesus wasn't giving gardening lessons, but He did refer to some common practices with which the disciples would have been familiar.

According to John 15:2, branches are supposed to _____.

According to John 15:2, branches that don't bear fruit are _____.

According to John 15:2, branches that do bear fruit are _____.

A branch that is attached to the vine is supposed to bear fruit. If it is not doing so, it needs attention! We have just highlighted two gardening techniques that are important to understand. But John 15:2 has been interpreted in different ways.

I want to keep this simple, but there are some very important details to consider.

Look at the two phrases in John 15:2 that describe the branches:

#1 — **<u>Every branch in Me</u>** that does not bear fruit

#2 — and **<u>every branch</u>** that bears fruit

Diagramming John 15:2 in Greek shows that these statements are parallel. Both sets of branches are "in Me," in Christ, belonging to Him, and having salvation. Some interpreters say that "in Me" could indicate an association with Christ but not salvation in Christ. Based on the teaching of the New Testament and the importance of the phrase "in Christ," I do not agree with this. For a review of what it means to be "in Christ" turn back to pages 39-41.

Keep in mind that Jesus is sharing His final words with His eleven disciples – Judas, the traitor, has already left the group – and these final words are His encouragement and directions for His closest friends. The eleven disciples are all "in Him."

Now look at the two phrases in John 15:2 and highlight what the Father, the Vinedresser, does to the branches:

#1 — Every branch in Me that does not bear fruit <u>He takes away</u>

#2 — and every branch that bears fruit <u>He prunes</u>

Can a branch – in Christ – lose her salvation due to unfruitfulness? Many think that is what Jesus taught. Based on all of Scripture and to be consistent in my understanding of the doctrine of salvation, I cannot agree with that interpretation. But if not that, then what?

Please look up the definition for the following words:

Takes away: Strong's #142

Greek word:

Greek definition:

Prunes: Strong's #2508

Greek word:

Greek definition:

> **The Greek verb αἴρω (*airò*) can mean "lift up"** as well as "take away," and it is sometimes argued that here it is a reference to the gardener "lifting up" (i.e., propping up) a weak branch so that it bears fruit again. In [John] Johannine usage the word occurs in the sense of "lift up" in 8:59 and 5:8–12, but in the sense of "remove" it is found in 11:39, 11:48, 16:22, and 17:15.[14]

We usually picture a vineyard with vines raised up on trellises, but there are other ways of growing them. In the Zondervan Pictorial Encyclopedia of the Bible, Schultz points out that "most of the vines in Palestine trail on the ground, because it is believed that the grapes ripen more slowly under the shadow of the leaves."[15]

I attended a class taught by Dr. Arnold Fruchtenbaum and had an opportunity to ask him specifically about John 15:2. He is a Messianic Jew who lived and studied in Israel and led countless tours throughout Israel. He told me that he had seen freestanding vines growing low to the ground with their branches raised up on rocks. He said this was still the way that Arabs grow their vines. Vines can also be trained on a vertical stake. Branches must be lifted up so that grape clusters do not rest on the ground, where they would contact the soil and be ruined.

I have been to Israel. I don't remember walking through a vineyard, but there was a moment when our tour guide pointed out some vines and commented on how close to the ground they were growing. He made the point that the closer to the ground the vine was, the more warmth from the ground it would receive, and this would produce sweeter grapes. But the branch on the ground does not produce grapes. It has to be raised up.

It makes so much sense to me that the Vinedresser would lift up a fruitless branch so that it will bear fruit.

What is the goal of the Vinedresser regarding both types of branches in John 15:2?

> Left to itself, a vine will produce a good deal of unproductive growth. For maximum fruitfulness extensive pruning is essential. This is a suggestive figure for the Christian life. The fruit of Christian service is never the result of allowing the natural energies and inclinations to run riot.[16]

Are you bearing fruit or do you need lifting up? Or is this a season of pruning in your life? What might our Father the Vinedresser cut away so that you will bear more fruit? Is there anything "running riot" and hindering your service to the Lord?

> Do let us believe that as the owner of a vine does everything to make the fruitage as rich and large as possible, the divine Husbandman will do all that is needed to make us bear more fruit. All He asks is that we set our heart's desire on it, entrust ourselves to His working and care, and joyfully look to Him to do His perfect work in us. God has set His heart on more fruit; Christ waits to work it in us; let us joyfully look up to our divine Husbandman and our heavenly Vine, to ensure our bearing more fruit.[17]

How does Jesus encourage His disciples in John 15:3?

The disciples are clean because they have believed Jesus' teachings. The disciples are clean because they have believed that Jesus is the Messiah, the Son of God.

Those who reject Jesus and His word are found in John 15:6. Many commentators state that the branches in John 15:2 are also referred to in John 15:6. But there's a difference in how they are described.

NKJ John 15:6 If anyone does not abide in Me, he is cast out as a branch and is withered; and they gather them and throw them into the fire, and they are burned.

How is the branch in John 15:6 described differently than the branches in John 15:2, and who handles the branches?

Jesus gives a lot of detail regarding what happens to the branch not abiding in Him. And it's not good.

His statement echoes Matthew 13:40-42. What is gathered, why is it gathered, and what happens to it?

How would you summarize Jesus' teaching regarding the different branches?

This has been a walk through the winter vineyard. The branches are all ready for the growing and fruit-bearing seasons! We'll enjoy examining a bountiful harvest of grapes in the next lesson.

LESSON 9

An Abundant Harvest

JOHN 15:1-17

Have you visited a vineyard during harvest time? I haven't yet, but I've always wanted to walk through the vines laden with bunches of grapes. As I have been studying John 15, I've researched viticulture – the culture and harvesting of grapes. Taking care of the vineyard so that it produces good quality fruit. I've learned that it is no easy task! One vineyard owner says:

> I have always stressed that great wines can only be produced from great grapes, and that one has to adapt all measures in the vineyard to the unpredictable and unstoppable impact of nature. We have to observe nature every day and react with respect for sustainability. So I live on the estate, in the middle of the vineyards, and can walk all the vineyards every week—harvest time and every day. I continuously know how our plants are doing and what needs to be done.[18]

Our Father God watches over His vineyard – of believers – with even more close attention and care than the vineyard owner quoted above. Our Father God knows every branch! Our Father God, the vinedresser, wants not just good fruit, but the highest quality fruit.

Please pray that the Holy Spirit will give you understanding of your role in bearing the best fruit.

How is this high-quality fruit produced in our lives, and what are the specific fruits that the Lord commands us to bear?

Please read John 15:1-17 below. Verses 1-8 are the illustration and verses 9-17 are the explanation. Highlight the following words: **abide, fruit, love,** and **command**. You can use the same color for all the words.

^NKJ **John 15:1-17** I am the true vine, and My Father is the vinedresser. ²Every branch in Me that does not bear fruit He takes away; and every branch that bears fruit He prunes, that it may bear more fruit. ³You are already clean because of the word which I have spoken to you. ⁴Abide in Me, and I in you. As the branch cannot bear fruit of itself, unless it abides in the vine, neither can you, unless you abide in Me. ⁵I am the vine, you are the branches. He who abides in Me, and I in him, bears much fruit; for without Me you can do nothing. ⁶If anyone does not abide in Me, he is cast out as a branch and is withered; and they gather them and throw them into the fire, and they are burned. ⁷If you abide in Me, and My words abide in you, you will ask what you desire, and it shall be done for you. ⁸By this My Father is glorified, that you bear much fruit; so you will be My disciples. ⁹As the Father loved Me, I also have loved you; abide in My love. ¹⁰If you keep My commandments, you will abide in My love, just as I have kept My Father's commandments and abide in His love. ¹¹These things I have spoken to you, that My joy may remain in you, and that your joy may be full. ¹²This is My commandment, that you love one another as I have loved you. ¹³Greater love has no one than this, than to lay down one's life for his friends. ¹⁴You are My friends if you do whatever I command you. ¹⁵No longer do I call you servants, for a servant does not know what his master is doing; but I have called you friends, for all things that I heard from My Father I have made known to you. ¹⁶You did not choose Me, but I chose you and appointed you that you should go and bear fruit, and that your fruit should remain, that whatever you ask the Father in My name He may give you. ¹⁷These things I command you, that you love one another.

Please look up the following word:

Abide: Strong's #3306

Greek word:

Greek definition:

Based on the passage above and the definition above, how is fruit produced in our lives?

There are several specifications about abiding in John 15:1-17. Please list these truths.

I don't think there is a passage of Scripture that I have turned to more often than the one we are studying. I turn to these words of Jesus because they are full of intimacy, encouragement, and instruction. They tell me who Jesus is and who I am. They give me rest, but they also remind me of my purpose.

Some of the things that Jesus tells His disciples, and us, are so obvious that it's surprising that He has to say them. But Jesus knows our humanity and forgetfulness and our independent attitudes.

So that we don't forget… please answer the following questions from John 15:1-17.

What does Jesus call Himself?

What does Jesus call His disciples?

How does a real branch growing in a real vineyard produce fruit?

What point about bearing fruit does Jesus make emphatically clear in John 15:5?

Before Jesus' death, His disciples remained with Him all the time. They listened to and obeyed His instructions. But Jesus was about to go away. Let me remind you again that this illustration of Jesus as the vine and disciples as branches is the focal point of His message in John 13:31-16:33. His entire message is about His gift of the indwelling Holy Spirit. If the Holy Spirit is in you, Jesus is in you, abiding in you, remaining in you.

What did Jesus promise in John 14:16-18?

Based on John 14:16-18, how does Jesus abide in us?

Jesus abides in us through His Holy Spirit. Amazing!

Now let's consider: How do we abide in Christ?

We've already looked at the Greek word **meno** *which means to remain, to stay, not to depart from, to continue to be with someone. It can mean to dwell, to live with someone permanently.*

We have a permanent home in Christ. If we think about being a branch attached to the vine, we know that life for the branch only comes from the vine. How did we get that life as a branch in the vine? By God's grace and our faith (Ephesians 2:8-9). How do we stay alive as a branch on the vine? By God's grace and our faith.

How do we abide in Christ? By God's grace and our faith. That's amazing too!

Walking by faith. Walking in the Spirit. Abiding in Christ. It's all the same thing.

Faith shows itself through obedience to the Lord, through submission to the Holy Spirit. That's just what Jesus talks about as He explains the illustration of the vine and branches.

What does Jesus say about obedience in John 15:10?

What mind-blowing truth did Jesus declare in John 15:9?

Considering these two verses together shows us that Jesus obeyed the Father, keeping all His commandments because: (1) the Father loves Him; and (2) Jesus loves His Father.

Considering our relationship to Jesus in light of these truths shows us that: (1) God the Father loves us as much as He loves Jesus! (2) Jesus loves us as much as God loves us! (3) We are to keep the Lord's commandments because of our love for Him.

What does Galatians 2:20 tell us that parallels with what we've been considering? (Note what we do and what Christ did.)

What does Galatians 3:14 tell us that also parallels what we've been studying in John 14 and 15?

Look at your highlights of John 15:1-17 again. What is the specific fruit that Jesus mentions that will be produced when we abide in Him?

It's time to pause and think about all these things in our own lives. Let's review it one more time. Please summarize what you have learned about who God is, who Jesus is, who you are, and what abiding is all about.

The sun is shining and it's time to check the fields. The branches are strong and much fruit is appearing in the vineyard. It's all because of the one, true, perfect vine. We'll look at this passage once more in the next lesson to see how very valuable the vine is.

NKJ **2 Peter 1:5-8** But also for this very reason, giving all diligence, add to your faith virtue, to virtue knowledge, ⁶to knowledge self-control, to self-control perseverance, to perseverance godliness, ⁷to godliness brotherly kindness, and to brotherly kindness love. ⁸For if these things are yours and abound, you will be neither barren nor unfruitful in the knowledge of our Lord Jesus Christ.

LESSON 10

The Valuable Vine

JOHN 15:8-17

The words of Jesus are so important. Each word and message gives us exactly what we need to hear. I'm not sure if the disciples realized that they were receiving Jesus' very last words of instruction to them, but we know it now.

This increases the gravity of His message even more.

―― ―― ――

Please ask the Holy Spirit to strengthen you to obey all that Jesus has commanded you to do.

―― ―― ――

Please read John 15:1-17.

What is the ultimate purpose of bearing fruit, according to John 15:8?

What has Jesus been saying over and over again in this last message? Note His statements in the verses below:

John 14:13

John 14:15 (write this whole verse)

John 14:21

John 14:23

John 14:31

John 15:9

John 15:10 (write this whole verse)

John 15:12

John 15:13

John 15:17

Love. Love God and love each other. Because God loves us and Jesus loves us. What will all that love look like? Heaven! But, we are being told to live it out on earth right now.

Maybe you noticed that John 14:15 and John 15:10 are like mirror-images of each other. <u>Read them again and highlight them in the list above.</u>

Loving Jesus will prompt us to keep His commands (John 14:15). Keeping His commands will result in abiding in His love (John 15:10). The following comment explains this well:

> The only natural conclusion from these virtually reversible statements is that they are so interrelated and inseparable that you cannot have one without the other. Moreover, once again the relationship of the disciple to Jesus in terms of obedience and love is modeled on the relationship of the Son to the Father.[19]

What is your reaction to Jesus' statements and the explanation above, regarding loving Him and keeping His commandments? Are you loving Jesus and keeping His commands? Are you keeping His commands and abiding in His love?

> Sometimes Christians get so busy figuring out how they should be loving God that they forget to love one another. In fact, a constant and genuine love for one another would be one way to show love for God.[20]

What did Jesus say in John 15:13 that indicated what He was about to do? Look at John 16:5 and John 16:17 and note whether the disciples understood what was about to happen.

I'm thankful for the work of the Holy Spirit who kept all of these words of Jesus in the mind of John! The disciples did not understand what Jesus was telling them at the time. But their lives were evidence that what He promised He fulfilled, and then the disciples understood His love for them.

How was this command eventually obeyed or expressed, according to the verses below?

Romans 16:4

Philippians 2:30

1 John 3:16

Jesus laid down His life for His friends. He laid down His life for you. He told the disciples and us to do the same. This may entail dying a martyr's death, but for most of us it doesn't.

How do you do what Jesus did, if you don't die? How do you obey His command to love like He did? What does this look like in your own life?

Let's get a few reminders of what love looks like. Record the description of love from 1 Corinthians 13:1-8.

Personalize Paul's prayer about love found in 1 Thessalonians 3:12-13 and rewrite it (and pray it) as your own prayer.

Jesus' whole message to His disciples was to encourage them and prepare them for their mission after His ascension to Heaven. What extremely encouraging declarations did He make in John 15:11-17?

Only Abraham had been called the friend of God. Now Jesus calls eleven men His friends! It was the start of something new, and you're His friend too, if you have believed in Him as your Savior.

One of the special privileges of being a friend of Jesus is the opportunity to ask Him for anything. Anything? Well, anything that is consistent with His nature and His will.

What was Jesus' promise in John 14:13-14?

What was Jesus' promise in John 15:7?

*Have you ever thought about the fact that before Jesus ascended into Heaven, no one had ever prayed **to Jesus?** Think about it. Prayers were offered to God in Heaven. Not Jesus on earth. Because we live after the time of Jesus' ascension, we've never experienced anything except Jesus being in Heaven. But there He was, face to face with His disciples, telling them that they could pray to Him. Surprise!*

What does Hebrews 4:14-16 teach us about praying?

Thank You Jesus.

He has more to say about praying which we will consider in a later lesson.

LESSON 11

Bad News

JOHN 15:18-25

We've just heard Jesus make the most personal, intimate declarations. His love for us is overwhelming. And we are to love others as He loves us. What a moment of tenderness.

But then the world and its hate burst into that moment. Jesus wasn't surprised about this and neither should we be.

Please pray to trust the Lord in the midst of hard trials.

Please read John 15:18-25.

*In the first few verses, the word **world** is used. It's the Greek word **kosmos** and "refers here to the unbelieving world of mankind, particularly those who are part of Satan's world system that is so hostile to God." [21]*

Let's start with the truths that Jesus laid out. What are the cold, hard facts that Jesus stated in the following verses?

John 15:18 – the world hated _____

John 15:19 – the world hates you because _____

John 15:20 – they persecuted Jesus, therefore they will _____

John 15:21 – they will do these things because _____

This is the first part of the bad news. The disciples will be treated as Jesus was. Because a servant is not greater than his master. To be associated with Jesus and to live according to the truths He taught is to be treated the way He was treated.

Some did respect and believe Jesus. Others rejected and despised Him. Record what you learn from the following verses:

These believed Jesus:

1. Matthew 9:27-28

2. Matthew 16:13-16

3. John 1: 49-50

4. John 4:40-42

These rejected Jesus:

1. Mark 11:18

2. Mark 14:61-64

3. Luke 11:53-54

4. John 19:14-15

Read John 15:18-21 again.

What does your perspective need to be regarding the negative reaction that some people will have toward you as you live according to Jesus' commands and example?

> The apostles should not be disturbed because of this so general hatred, imagining that they have themselves provoked it, and believing that they see in it the proof that they are on a wrong path: "but take courage; it is because of Me." Because of My name, says Jesus; that is, because of the revelation of My person which you have received, and which you will declare to them.[22]

Please read John 15:22-25. Fill in the blanks and answer the questions below:

John 15:22: If I had not come and spoken to _____ , they would have no sin, but now they have _____ for their sin.

John 15:23-24: He who hates Me hates _____ also. If I had not done among them the _____, they would have no sin; but now they have _____ and also _____ both _____.

- To whom did Jesus come and speak? (Base your answer on this passage and the previous passages in this lesson.)

- Why did they have no excuse for their sin?

- What was their reaction to Jesus?

> The former sin of Israel – its long resistance to God – would have been forgiven, if it had not now crowned all by the rejection of Jesus as He came as Savior and bore testimony to Himself as such.
>
> If the testimony which Jesus bore to Himself did not succeed in enlightening them, His works ought at least to have procured credence for His testimony.[23]

This was the blindness and sin of the Jews. It was "the rejection of God's gracious revelation, rebellion against God, decisive preference for darkness rather than light."[24] They would be held accountable for their rejection of Jesus.

Jesus grieved over the sin of the Jews, knowing what would come as a consequence.

What did He say would happen according to Matthew 23:37-39?

What would happen according to Luke 19:41-44?

What was the very sad truth that Jesus declared in John 15:25?

He was quoting from Psalm 35 as He referred to the Jews who hated Him.

Highlight below what Jesus quoted in John 15:25.

NKJ Psalm 35:19-20 Let them not rejoice over me who are wrongfully my enemies; nor let them wink with the eye who hate me without a cause. For they do not speak peace, but they devise deceitful matters against the quiet ones in the land.

There is much in the prophecy of Isaiah 53:3-9 that tells us what Jesus would suffer. Note that which relates to what we've been studying.

What was acknowledged about Jesus, according to the verses below?

By Pontius Pilate and Herod – Luke 23:14-15

By the criminal on the cross - Luke 23:41

By the Roman officer (centurion) at the cross - Luke 23:47

Jesus was born in Bethlehem, in Judea, in Israel. He grew up in Nazareth and attended every festival in Jerusalem. He walked in the streets of the towns and traveled throughout all the countryside. He obeyed every command of the Lord. He came to the Jews. His people. Jesus was a Jew. He came as their Messiah but they would not accept that He was **the One who had been promised.**

Because the Jewish leaders (chief priests, scribes, Pharisees, Sadducees) rejected Jesus, they led the people to reject Him as well. All Israel went astray and sinned against the Lord and His Messiah.

All Israel suffered the consequence of this sin when the Romans attacked Jerusalem in 70 A.D. The temple was destroyed and has never been rebuilt. The Jews were dispersed again and have been scattered all over the world ever since. 1948 brought about a tremendous change for the Jews when Israel became an independent, sovereign nation.

But the real change will come when the leaders of Israel recognize their sin of rejection of their Messiah and lead the nation to repentance. Zechariah 12:10 tells us that Israel will mourn for the one whom they pierced and there will be great mourning all over the land.

Not until Israel repents of this sin will Jesus come back to the earth to reign as Messiah. The Bible tells us about other details that will happen before Israel repents, but that's another study!

Please pray for any Jews that the Lord brings to mind at this time. That the Lord would open their eyes to know that Jesus is the One promised by the Lord throughout the Old Testament. That they would acknowledge their need for forgiveness and know that Jesus gave His life as an atonement for their sin.

Let us obey Jesus and be those of these verses in Psalm 35, even in the hard times of being persecuted for His name's sake:

^{NKJ} **Psalm 35:27-28**   Let them shout for joy and be glad, who favor my righteous cause; and let them say continually, "Let the LORD be magnified, who has pleasure in the prosperity of His servant." And my tongue shall speak of Your righteousness and of Your praise all the day long.

LESSON 12

Good Works

JOHN 15:26-16:7

When we love Jesus and abide in His love, and love the way He loves… there will still be those around us who despise and reject Him. And they will despise and reject us. Jesus has told us this will happen and what we are to think about it. He also told us how to respond.

What did Jesus tell us to do in Matthew 5:11-16?

How are we supposed to do that? Jesus didn't intend for us to handle it on our own, alone.

———

Please pray that the Holy Spirit will make His work known to you.

———

Please read John 15:26-John 16:7.

What three things does Jesus reveal about the Holy Spirit in John 15:26?

His titles:

His origin:

His work:

Jesus had been on the earth, testifying to His identity and to His Father's kingdom. He was about to depart, but there would still be testimonies about who Jesus is.

Based on John 15:26-27, who would testify to the identity of Jesus after He was gone?

Do you see that this means that the Holy Spirit testifies about Jesus through us, and we testify about Jesus through the Holy Spirit working in us? Remember the vine and branches? We bear fruit as the life of the vine flows through us. Let's think about this using a different illustration that Jesus gave us.

According to John 4:10-14, what is the gift of God that Jesus gives? What happens when you receive this gift?

According to John 7:37-39, what did Jesus offer? And to what was He referring?

When Jesus spoke to the woman at the well, He testified to her of His identity as the Messiah (John 4:25-26). He offered her living water, which we saw in John 7:39 was a reference to the Holy Spirit. When we obey Jesus, and love as He loved, and bear fruit, that's the Holy Spirit working in us and through us. Living water springs up from the well of the Spirit and flows out through our lives to quench the thirsts of dying souls.

With whom will the disciples be sharing this testimony and living water? What will happen? Look at the context of Jesus' words. Base your answer on John 15:16-16:3.

Jesus prepared His disciples. These things – these persecutions – were a certainty. Hostility would be hurled against His witnesses, as real stones were thrown, as they were beaten and put in prison, and as death threats were made against them. Jesus' comfort and encouragement was that He would be with them, because He was sending His Holy Spirit to be in them.

Prepared with this knowledge, and emboldened by the Holy Spirit, the disciples testified. They turned the world upside down according to some Thessalonian city leaders! They testified to the identity of Jesus as the Messiah, the Savior of the World, the One and Only Son of God. They did this through their miracles, preaching, writing, lives and deaths. Many died a martyr's death. Many believers throughout the history of the church have been persecuted or killed for their faith.

> There is a responsibility resting on all Christians to bear their witness to the facts of saving grace. They cannot evade this. But the really significant witness is that of the Holy Spirit, for He alone can bring home to the hearts of men the truth and the significance of all this.[25]

What do you need to trust the Holy Spirit to do in and through you? Be specific.

Let's look a few more important things from Jesus' message at this point.

Highlight references to, including pronouns, **Jesus, the Father,** and **the Holy Spirit.**

Highlight phrases which include: **send.**

^{NKJ} **John 15:26 - 16:7** But when the Helper comes, whom I shall send to you from the Father, the Spirit of truth who proceeds from the Father, He will testify of Me. ²⁷And you also will bear witness, because you have been with Me from the beginning. **John 16:1** These things I have spoken to you, that you should not be made to stumble. ²They will put you out of the synagogues; yes, the time is coming that whoever kills you will think that he offers God service. ³And these things they will do to you because they have not known the Father nor Me. ⁴But these things I have told you, that when the time comes, you may remember that I told you of them. And these things I did not say to you at the beginning, because I was with you. ⁵But now I go away to Him who sent Me, and none of you asks Me, "Where are You going?" ⁶But because I have said these things to you, sorrow has filled your heart. ⁷Nevertheless I tell you the truth. It is to your advantage that I go away; for if I do not go away, the Helper will not come to you; but if I depart, I will send Him to you.

Jesus speaks with authority, doesn't He? He knows what He is talking about!

Please notice some facts which give evidence of our triune God. He is three-in-one.

Who sent Jesus? _____

Who sent the Holy Spirit? _____

The Holy Spirit proceeds from whom? _____

To whom did Jesus say He was going? _____

What was the advantage to us of Jesus going away?

While this plan to send the Holy Spirit was explained by Jesus right before His departure, the disciples should have known about the reality of the Spirit from their Old Testament scriptures.

Record the truths about the Holy Spirit from the verses below:

Genesis 1:2

Job 33:4

Psalm 139:7

Isaiah 11:1-2

Understanding the Trinity is definitely beyond our full comprehension! Let's just be amazed and in awe of our great triune God. He is holy, holy, holy. God in three persons. Blessed Trinity.

Look at Isaiah 48:16 where God the Son is speaking. Who does He say sent Him?

Wow. God the Father and God the Spirit sent God the Son – Jesus – to earth, to Israel, to die on the cross. Then, upon His return to Heaven, God the Son and God the Father sent God the Spirit to be in and with all who believe in Jesus.

What did Jesus want the disciples to do with this information that He was giving them, according to John 16:4?

Keep this in mind. Think about this promise. Remember. Don't forget about the Holy Spirit.

What is something about the Holy Spirit that has been brought to your attention in this lesson that you need to remember? Look over this lesson and note at least one meaningful idea.

There's more to learn about the Spirit in the next lesson!

LESSON 13

The Work of the Holy Spirit

JOHN 16:8-15

When you've got something good that you're happy with, it's really hard to imagine how something else can be better. I'm never eager to swap out my computer or smartphone for a newer model. I've gotten used to the way the old one works! And now I have to learn some newfangled gadget. Newfangled – it's a real word.

Jesus is going to explain to the disciples just how great this newfangled situation is going to be for them. Here comes the Holy Spirit and He is amazing!

Please pray that the Holy Spirit will do His work in you.

Please read John 16:8-15.

List every observation you can make about the Holy Spirit from these verses. Try to list at least 10 details. (Just list them, you don't have to explain them.)

Was one of your observations the truth that the Holy Spirit is referred to as "He"? This means that He is a person. He is not an "it." Just as we observed in the previous lesson, the Holy Spirit is one of the three persons of our triune God.

*Let's stop right there and consider that the Holy Spirit is sent **from** God the Father and sent **by** God the Son. And the Holy Spirit is God.*

Note a few attributes of God with which you are familiar. Then consider that these same attributes belong to the Holy Spirit. I've given you an example.

God is:
omnipresent

The Holy Spirit is:
omnipresent

The Holy Spirit convinces individuals of their sin. What does that mean regarding your involvement in sharing the gospel? What is your responsibility?

The Holy Spirit convicts the world of righteousness because Jesus went to the Father and we see Him no more. What does this mean?

> Christ's return to Heaven, to be welcomed by the Father is the ultimate proof that He is the perfect pattern of righteousness that God accepts. The Holy Spirit will convict unbelievers of their failure to accept the standard of righteousness that God approves – the righteousness exemplified in the person of Christ, who remains the ultimate standard of righteousness for the world.[26]

Only Jesus could go to Heaven on His own merit! No one else is good enough. The Holy Spirit convicts individuals of this.

The third area of conviction is about the judgment which will come to unbelievers. Jesus said: "the ruler of this world is judged." That's Satan. And if he stands judged, condemned, and will face the wrath of God, so will everyone else who is against Jesus. "Few people cherish an intimate association with a loser. Satan is a loser, and those who unite themselves with him through sin and unbelief will be lost as well."[27]

Review the facts about the Holy Spirit that we've covered this far. Fill in the blanks below with one word. It's a different word in each blank.

The Holy Spirit is _____.

The Holy Spirit convicts the world of _____.

The Holy Spirit convicts the world of _____.

The Holy Spirit convicts the world of _____.

These three areas of conviction show us the gospel.[28]

1. *The sinner needs to see his state of sin from God's perspective.*

2. *He needs to know that the righteousness Christ demonstrated provides the basis for salvation.*

3. *The sinner must be reminded that if he refuses Christ's provision, he faces certain judgment.*

How did the Holy Spirit convict you of your need for salvation through Jesus Christ? Was one of these areas a focal point in your understanding of the gospel?

What was the bad news and the good news that Jesus gave the disciples, according to John 16:12-15?

How does this apply to you today? How does the Holy Spirit guide you into all truth?

What happened to fulfill these promises of Jesus? First, He had to go away, that is, die on the cross. What happened after that, according to Matthew 28:5-7?

And then what happened, according to Acts 1:2-9?

And then what happened, according to Acts 2:1-6?

And then what happened while Peter was preaching to Cornelius, according to Acts 10:42-48?

The promised gift of the Holy Spirit was poured out in a way that had never happened before. Jesus' death, resurrection, and ascension made the way for the Helper to come. To say that it was exciting is an understatement!

The giving and sending of the Holy Spirit was a fulfillment of the New Covenant promise given through Ezekiel 36:26-27 and Ezekiel 37:5, 9, 14. What does God do that no person can do for themselves?

The Holy Spirit gives life and seals the deal. How did Paul declare this in Ephesians 1:13-14 and Titus 3:4-6?

What difference does the Holy Spirit make in our lives, according to Romans 8:1-2 and Romans 8:9-17?

The Holy Spirit makes all the difference in the world, and all the difference in eternity, doesn't He? We don't have life without Him!

Praise God and thank Jesus for giving us the amazing gift of His indwelling Holy Spirit.

LESSON 14

A Time of Sorrow

JOHN 16:16-22

Picture this. It's late in the evening after the special Passover meal. The disciples are with Jesus and He has been sharing some surprising things with them. They have asked a few questions, but for the most part, they are listening intently to what Jesus has been saying. They are trying to understand what He is talking about.

But they don't quite get it.

Please pray for endurance and God's perspective during challenging and heart-breaking times.

Please read John 16:16-22.

What is Jesus' statement that causes confusion? It's repeated seven times in this passage.

Using two colors – one for the phrase Jesus repeated and one for the phrase in the disciples' questions – highlight the repeated statement.

NKJ **John 16:16-19** "A little while, and you will not see Me; and again a little while, and you will see Me, because I go to the Father." ¹⁷Then some of His disciples said among themselves, "What is this that He says to us, 'A little while, and you will not see Me; and again a little while, and you will see Me;' and, 'because I go to the Father?'" ¹⁸They said therefore, "What is this that He says, 'A little while?' We do not know what He is saying." ¹⁹Now Jesus knew that they desired to ask Him, and He said to them, "Are you inquiring among yourselves about what I said, 'A little while, and you will not see Me; and again a little while, and you will see Me?'"

> The disciples' difficulty centered on the phrase "a little while." They continued asking one another the meaning of this key phrase. They had to confess their own lack of comprehension of Jesus' words. They simply had no idea what He was talking about. If the disciples had difficulty understanding the teaching of Jesus when they were in His presence, it is not surprising that we have difficulty with some of His teaching 2,000 years later.²⁹

That's nice to know! But let's keep it really simple. We already know what was about to happen and that will help us understand what Jesus was saying in John 16:16.

"In a little while" – *in a few hours, a short period of time*

"you will not see Me" – *Jesus would be taken away, crucified, and buried*

"and again a little while" – *another short period of time*

"you will see Me" – *Jesus would be with the disciples again, after His resurrection*

Look at John 16:32, which shows that Jesus was aware of how soon He would be arrested. Note His comment about the time.

We know the rest of the story, and we know what happened right after the Last Supper. Even though Jesus had been telling the disciples that He would suffer, be killed, and be raised on the third day (Matthew 16:21), this information just didn't make sense to them.

Jesus explained things with an analogy. Using three colors, highlight: (1) any mention of timing; (2) any mention of sorrow; (3) any mention of joy.

^{NKJ} **John 16:20-22** "Most assuredly, I say to you that you will weep and lament, but the world will rejoice; and you will be sorrowful, but your sorrow will be turned into joy. ²¹A woman, when she is in labor, has sorrow because her hour has come; but as soon as she has given birth to the child, she no longer remembers the anguish, for joy that a human being has been born into the world. ²²Therefore you now have sorrow; but I will see you again and your heart will rejoice, and your joy no one will take from you."

This passage of scripture was given to me when I was pregnant with my second child. I was tired of being pregnant; I was uncomfortable and impatient as I waited for my baby girl to be born. I needed an attitude adjustment and a sweet friend wrote these verses out on little pink paper booties for me. The Lord used them to give me peace and patience, with the anticipation of the great joy that I would have when Emily was born.

Based on your highlighting and keeping John 16:16-19 in mind, answer the following questions:

What would the disciples experience for a little while? What would cause this?

What would be the ultimate outcome after a short time?

What promise was repeated in John 16:16 and 16:22?

The resurrection of Jesus Christ is a historical fact, even though there are some who claim it's just a legend. There are no skeletons in God's closet. No body in the tomb.

Who saw Jesus after His resurrection, according to the verses below? Note any details which would indicate that Jesus appeared in bodily form.

Mark 16:9-14

Luke 24:33-43

John 20:26-29

Not only did Jesus tell the disciples that they would see Him again, He also told them that He would return to the earth one day. Jesus is coming back!

But before Jesus returns to earth, He will return in the clouds to rapture His Bride, the church. This is the gathering of all who have believed in Jesus since His resurrection and they will be taken to heaven in resurrected, glorified bodies.

Note the details about this gathering described in 1 Thessalonians 4:14-18.

According to 1 Timothy 6:12-16, what is our behavior to be while waiting for Jesus? How is Jesus described in this passage?

How is Jesus' return to earth described in Revelation 19:11-16 and 19? Note what you learn about Jesus and about His actions.

And finally, in the New Jerusalem, when all evil has been vanquished, according to Revelation 22:3-5, who will we see? What is the description of this place?

Jesus told His disciples that in a little while their hearts would rejoice and no one would be able to take their joy away. We can begin the rejoicing now! Our joy is only going to become greater and greater.

Peter experienced everything Jesus talked about. The death of Jesus. Sorrow. The resurrection of Jesus. Amazement and joy. The ascension of Jesus. Anticipation of His return.

What did Peter tell us to do, according to 1 Peter 1:6-9?

If you are experiencing a time of sorrow and grief, do you realize that it is temporary and short when compared to the eternity of joy you will have when you are with Jesus? Do you need any attitude adjustments regarding your perspectives on your suffering?

Here are some questions to consider:

Do you believe what Jesus promised – that you will see Him?

Do you believe that the sorrow and waiting will only be for a little while?

Are you hoping for the future joys that have been promised to you?

Are you longing to see Jesus because of your love for Him?

Now would be a good time to read the first part of Jesus' message again – John 14.

LESSON 15

Ask the Father

JOHN 16:22-28

The passage we will look at in this lesson includes several very important aspects of our faith. At the same time, it includes a few things that are challenging to understand. Commentaries offer various interpretations. I don't want to get bogged down in the difficulties. I do want us to rejoice — as Jesus tells us we will — in the precious truths that we will see.

Please ask our Father God to help you understand the privilege you have to talk to Him.

We need to do a little review. Please read John 16:16-28.

According to John 16:16-17: The disciples said among themselves: "what's He saying to us?"

According to John 16:19: Jesus knew that _____, and

Jesus said: "Are you _____ among yourselves about what I said…?"

According to John 16:23: Jesus said: "In that day _____."

And "Whatever _____, He will give you."

I hope this begins to emphasize that there is a lot of discussion about asking. Some of it has to do with asking Jesus to explain what He is saying. Some of it has to do with asking in prayer.

The time was coming when Jesus would speak with His disciples in a different way. How had He been speaking to them and what would be different, based on John 16:25?

Please remember the promise just given in John 16:12-14. What would the Holy Spirit do?

Before Jesus' death and resurrection, the disciples were trying to understand but were limited by their basic humanity. But afterwards! When they received the Holy Spirit at Pentecost, there was a brand new situation!

Paul talks about this in 1 Corinthians 2:11-14. What does the natural man know? How can someone know the things of God?

Consider these truths and conversations you may have about spiritual matters. Who will be able to understand what you're talking about?

Lest you think that it's pointless to share spiritual truth and the gospel with unbelievers, please note the very important exhortation in Romans 10:13-17.

Let's return to the instructions Jesus gave to His disciples regarding prayer. His specific statements are quoted below.

Highlight: **ask** and **My name.**

John 16:23: Whatever you ask the Father in My name He will give you.

John 16:24: Until now you have asked nothing in My name.

    Ask, and you will receive, that your joy may be full.

John 16:26: In that day you will ask in My name, and I do not say to you that I shall pray the Father for you; ²⁷for the Father Himself loves you, because you have loved Me, and have believed that I came forth from God.

*This is not a **pattern for prayer**. It's a teaching on the **nature of prayer.** Each statement directs us to pray to our Father God.*

Why do we have the privilege of calling God our Father, and the privilege of praying directly and boldly to Him, based on John 16:26? Make sure you note the importance of what you believe about Jesus.

Perhaps this isn't anything new to you. Perhaps you have been a believer for long enough to have enjoyed this privilege of the open door to God's throne. But this was all new for the disciples. They had been with Jesus and had talked to Him about God in Heaven. They had asked Jesus how to pray and learned to say, "our Father." But they had never asked the Father to hear their prayers because they believed in Jesus as His Son, the Messiah, and their Savior.

That day was coming!

When Jesus was no longer with the disciples, the Holy Spirit would be with them, indwelling them and giving them life. What does Romans 8:14-17 tell us about this, and how does it relate to the comments above about prayer?

> The disciples must not be led to think that Jesus has to persuade the Father to answer their prayers: the Father is only too ready to do so because, as Jesus has assured them of His own love, so they may be assured of the Father's direct and personal love for them. Thanks to their loving and believing reception of Jesus, they have received "authority to become God's children" (John 1:12), and as children they have direct access to the Father with the confidence that He welcomes them and gladly attends to their requests.[30]

Turn to your Father in Heaven now, and talk to Him about whatever is on your heart. He is available to listen, love you, and respond to you.

The passage we've been considering has one sentence that extends from heaven to earth and back again. It's Jesus' summary of His life.

Please write out John 16:28. Jesus said:

There are four statements that relate to four critical doctrinal truths about Jesus. We must know, believe, and defend these truths. Fill in the blanks below based on John 16:28.

1. **Jesus' origin:** He was sent to the earth, from Heaven, from _____.

In this statement we see Jesus' deity, His eternality, and His obedience to the Father.

2. **Jesus' incarnation:** He came _____.

Here we see His self-sacrificing love, His humility, His servanthood, and His humanity.

3. **Jesus' crucifixion:** He was going to _____.

This indicates His imminent suffering, His death, and His voluntary sacrifice.

4. **Jesus' ascension:** He was going to _____.

His sacrifice as a perfect sinless substitute for us was accepted; He rose from the dead with a glorified body; He ascended into Heaven where He sits at the right hand of God the Father.

> Here we have the great movement of salvation. It is a twofold movement, from heaven to earth and back again. Christ's heavenly origin is important, else He could not be the Savior of men. But His heavenly destination is also important, for it witnesses to the Father's seal on the Son's saving work.[31]

Oh, we've got to do some singing and celebrating for all that Jesus has done for us! Here's an oldie for some of you. I remember when it was new to me!

Lord, I Lift Your Name on High [32]

Lord I lift Your name on high
Lord I love to sing Your praises
I'm so glad You're in my life
I'm so glad You came to save us

You came from heaven to earth to show the way
From the earth to the cross, my debt to pay
From the cross to the grave, from the grave to the sky
Lord I lift Your name on high

LESSON 16

Never Alone

JOHN 16:29-33

Things are really clicking now! The plan is coming together. The team is ready to go out and do what they've been trained to do. At least, that's what they think.

---

*Please pray that the Holy Spirit will comfort you
and enable you to press on in your witness for Jesus Christ.*

Please read John 16:29-33.

There will be a few more comments made between Jesus and His disciples before His death, but these are the last words that He will share with them one on one. If they have been walking and talking, they are probably close to the Garden of Gethsemane. Jesus will go and pray alone, and then be arrested and imprisoned and tried during the night.

The disciples think they understand Jesus now. What do they say they are sure of, according to John 16:30? Note their three declarations.

These declarations indicate that the disciples believed that Jesus was from God. Because He knew everything, including their thoughts, He was omniscient. He didn't even need them to ask Him questions because He knew what they were thinking! God is omniscient. So they believed He was from God and was God.

That was a big deal. A critical confession on the part of the disciples.

But they needed to brace themselves for Jesus' response.

What did He say that was a sobering prediction, according to John 16:31-32?

It was time. Jesus would finish the work His Father gave Him to do alone. But not alone – more on that later.

Please note the statements that refer to Jesus suffering alone:

Psalm 38:11-12

Zechariah 13:7

Matthew 26:39-40

Mark 14:50-52

> The voice of the mob was sounding in the streets. Judas was coming. The disciples could not hear these ominous sounds and were still complacent about Judas. But Jesus knew that the storm would break within the hour. "Ye shall be scattered," He warned, "every man to his own." The bond that held them together was about to be severed. Each one, thinking only of his personal safety, would run off into the night, making for his own home as fast as he could. How much they needed to beware of the fleeting emotion of the moment.[33]

They had the best intentions. But they didn't have everything they needed to endure what was coming. The Holy Spirit had been promised but did not indwell them yet.

Perhaps this night of fear and hiding and denial showed them their weaknesses. Sometimes we have to be humbled before we realize we need help.

Take this opportunity to consider if there is an area of your life and your faith in which you are over-confident. Do you say "I can handle it myself" or "I would never…."?

> Jesus was the loneliest man that ever lived. All other forms of human solitude were concentrated in His. He knew the pain of unappreciated aims, unaccepted love, unbelieved teachings, a heart thrown back upon itself. No man understood Him, no man knew Him, no man deeply and thoroughly loved Him or sympathized with Him, and He dwelt apart. He felt the pain of solitude more sharply than sinful men do. Perfect purity is keenly susceptible; a heart fully charged with love is wounded sore when the love is thrown back, and all the more sorely the more unselfish it is.[34]

Jesus knew that His closest friends would desert Him. Because of that, a magnificent statement of His intimacy with His Father and His faith in Him was shared.

What did Jesus say regarding not being alone, according to John 16:32?

Jesus had already been sharing the truths of the intimate relationship He has with His Father.

Note the relationship between Jesus and the Father from the following verses:

John 14:7

John 14:10-11

John 14:23

John 15:9

John 15:10

John 15:23

John 16:5

John 16:15

The Father was always with Jesus. Until that terrible dark time when He bore our sins on the cross, He had never experienced any separation from God the Father. The pain of that time was excruciating.

What did Jesus say in those dark hours, according to Matthew 27:46?

What did Jesus say that showed that the time of separation was over, according to Luke 23:46?

Three days later, what did the power of God the Father do, according to Ephesians 1:19-20?

After His ascension, Jesus was with His Father, side by side, once again!

Jesus depended on the presence of His Father in the most terrible time of His life. There is nothing you will face that will be worse than Jesus' crucifixion and temporary separation from His Father.

What promises has Jesus given you that you can depend on at all times? Write them in first person as declarations of what you believe.

Matthew 28:20

John 14:16-18

Hebrews 13:5

*There are, of course, many, many more promises regarding God's presence, comfort, grace, and strength for us during all the days of our lives no matter the circumstances. But the verses above have the idea of Jesus being **with** us.*

He stays with us. Abides with us. And we are not alone.

LESSON 17

Be of Good Cheer!

JOHN 16:33

*While the last words of Jesus are **His last words** and that makes them loaded with emotion and a sober declaration, they are also tremendous words of encouragement and hope. Jesus covered a lot of territory in one brief sentence.*

―――

Please pray that the Holy Spirit will remind you of the things Jesus has taught.

―――

Please write John 16:33. This would be a great verse to memorize.

Let's look briefly at all the topics He covered; then we will come back to each one.

<u>**These things I have spoken to you...**</u> – *He taught the disciples so much during their three years together, but this phrase is referring to the message we have been studying in John 14, 15, and 16.*

<u>**...That in Me...**</u> - *Don't forget how important the phrase "in Me" is.*

<u>**...you may have peace...**</u> - *This is not wishful thinking. Jesus intended for us to have real peace as a result of believing and living by what He has just shared.*

<u>**...In the world...**</u> - *We are still in the world. But this phrase reminds us that the world is our temporary place of residence. This world is not our home.*

<u>**...you will have tribulation...**</u> - *This is a certainty. Tribulation, trouble, suffering, heartache, pain. All of this will come upon us in one form or another because we live in a fallen world, among those who reject Jesus and reject us. And the ruler of this world hates us too.*

<u>**...but be of good cheer...**</u> - *This is such an encouraging thing to say. Try to imagine hearing Jesus say it. Don't skip over this simple little phrase. What a wonderful biblical exhortation! Jesus said it to His disciples. He is saying it to you. And you can say it to other believers.*

...I have overcome the world! – *Jesus is victorious! He has overcome every temptation, every obstacle, every enemy.*

Now let's go a little deeper into each phrase.

These things I have spoken to you... - What are the topics that Jesus has just spoken to the disciples about? List them briefly according to the verses below:

John 13:31

John 13:34

John 14:2-3

John 14:6

John 14:16-17

John 15:5

John 15:15

John 15:20-21

John 16:7

John 16:23-24

...That in Me... - What does it mean to be "in Christ"? Look at pages 39-41 for a review of this concept. What is your favorite verse regarding being in Christ?

...you may have peace... - What did Jesus say in John 14:27?

Please review and summarize what you learned about peace when we studied this verse in Lesson 7, pages 42-43.

Consider the topics listed above that Jesus talked about. How did He give His peace to the disciples and us?

...In the world you will have tribulation... - We know this is true! What were the specific situations that Jesus told the disciples they would experience? Note them according to the verses below:

John 15:19-20

John 16:2-3

What other types of tribulation did the disciples experience? What happened to James and Peter, according to Acts 12:1-5?

What did John experience, and why, according to Revelation 1:9?

...but be of good cheer... - *This phrase is from the New King James version. I like it. But the encouragement given in other translations is just as comforting. Be courageous! (CSB) Take heart! (ESV) Take courage! (NAS) The Greek word used is **tharseō**, a verb, that is only used as an imperative command in the New Testament, and only used by the Lord.*

Note the reason that Jesus told the following people to cheer up:

Matthew 9:2

Matthew 9:22

Mark 6:48-51

Mark 10:46-52

Paul was also told the same thing, according to Acts 23:11. Who said what to him?

How would you summarize the reason that we can be courageous?

If you need a little more assurance of why we can be of good cheer, Jesus' last words guarantee that He is going to take care of everything.

...I have overcome the world!

Please look up the following word:

Overcome: Strong's #3528

Greek word:

Greek definition:

Every believer is assured of victory in Jesus because He has conquered the world, its sin, and its ruler.

How did He do it? What did He win? How do we benefit?

Note what you learn from the verses below:

Galatians 1:4

Colossians 1:13-14

Colossian 2:13-15

1 John 5:4-5

Praise God for sending His Son! Praise Jesus for His defeat over sin and Satan and death! Praise God that we are on His team and enjoy the benefits of Jesus' victory!

How are you encouraged and cheered up by Jesus' victory? How does His victory impact your daily life and activities? Is there anything challenging you to which you need to apply His overcoming power?

I get up very early when I am away and writing Bible studies. I love to see the sunrise over the ocean, but what I really want to see is the pre-sunrise show. I love seeing the black morning sky with stars fade away as the orange glow of the sun begins to break over the horizon. Clouds give an abstract, artistic flair to the view. And sometimes it is just totally clear. And beautiful.

As I have been working on this verse, I've had a front row seat to one of those mornings. I think it's a good illustration of John 16:33. Because the sun is definitely going to rise, I know the dark sky will fade away. The glow of the orange sky tells me that the sun is coming. And eventually, its brightness will be overwhelming and change everything.

Jesus knew that He would defeat Satan and sin through His death on the cross and His resurrection. The Son rising was even more certain than our daily sunrise. The disciples could be of good cheer because of all of Jesus' promises to them. We can too.

Please write John 16:33 once again, perhaps from memory this time.

Special Note

There is one more review lesson in this workbook. Then you will have concluded the study of the last message of Jesus. He will soon face the suffering and glorification that He has been telling the disciples about.

This particular study ends here, but the rest of the story can be found in my study on Luke 22-24 entitled: ***Believe in Me — The Death and Resurrection of Jesus Christ.***

LESSON 18

Our Inheritance

JOHN 13:31-16:33

This study has taken an in-depth look at Jesus' last message to His disciples. I have gained a greater understanding of the timing and intensity of these truths. Jesus made sure His disciples knew these things before His death.

You might consider this as Jesus' "last will and testament." It was His will – His command. It was His testament – His declaration of who He is and what He would do. The inheritance we receive from this message is greater than anything we could receive on earth.

I hope you have enjoyed this time we have had together studying God's word. This has been, for me, a time of abiding in Christ.

I like to conclude my studies with the words of Scripture and your response to them, rather than your response to my words.

So please take the time now to read and hear the "last will and testament" of Jesus. Use the rest of this page to make notes of what He has said that stands out to you now. Perhaps the two columns below will help you capture key concepts.

Please read John 13:31-16:33.

Do This: **Know This:**

Endnotes

1. Study note on John 13:30 in NET Bible. Biblical Studies Press, 2003.
2. Sailhammer, John H., NIV Compact Bible Commentary. (Grand Rapids, Zondervan, 1994), 493.
3. Laney, J. Carl, *John*. Moody Gospel Commentary Series, ed. Paul Enns. (Chicago, Moody Press, 1992), 249.
4. Boice, James Montgomery, *The Gospel of John, Volume 4*. (Grand Rapids, Baker Books, 1999), 1051-1054.
5. Carson, D. A., *The Farewell Discourse and Final Prayer of Jesus*. (Grand Rapids, Baker Books, 1980), 25.
6. Borchert, Gerald L., *John 12-21, Vol. 25B*. The New American Commentary Series, ed. E. Ray Clendenen. (Nashville, B & H Publishing Group, 2002), 105.
7. https://popularhymns.com/when-we-all-get-to-heaven
8. Phillips, John. *Exploring the Gospels: John*. (Neptune, Loizeaux Brothers, 1989), 270.
9. Macarthur, J. and R. Mayhue, editors. *Biblical Doctrine: A Systematic Summary of Biblical Truth*. (Wheaton, Crossway, 2017), 602-603.
10. Hendrikson, William. *The Gospel of John*. (Grand Rapids, Baker Book House, 1987), 287.
11. Hendrikson, 288.
12. Study note on John 14:29 in NET Bible. Biblical Studies Press, 2003.
13. Boice, 1157.
14. Study note on John 15:2 in NET Bible. Biblical Studies Press, 2003.
15. Tenney, Merrill C., editor. *The Zondervan Pictorial Encyclopedia of the Bible*. (Grand Rapids, Zondervan Publishing House, 1975), s.v. "Vine, Vineyard," by A. C. Schultz, 882-884.
16. Morris, Leon. *The Gospel According to John*. The New International Commentary on the New Testament, ed. F. F. Bruce. (Grand Rapids, W. E. Eerdmans Publishing Co., 1984), 670.
17. Murray, Andrew. *The True Vine*. (Chicago, Moody Press, 1997), 25.
18. 2008 Harvest Winemakers' Blog, *As the Tuscan Harvest Ends, we Recognize our Staff's Hard Work* by Barbara Kronenberg-Widmer. https://www.winespectator.com/articles/as-the-tuscan-harvest-ends-we-recognize-our-staffs-hard-work-15798
19. Borchert, 146.
20. Gangel, Kenneth O. *John*. Holman New Testament Commentary, ed. Max Anders. (Nashville, B & H Publishing Group, 2000), 285.
21. Laney, 279.
22. Godet, Frederic Louis. *Gospel of John, vol. 2*. Collected Works of Frederic Louis Godet, Public Domain, (North Haven, CT, 2022), 212.
23. Godet, 212.
24. Carson, D. A., *The Gospel According to John*. (Grand Rapids, William B. Eerdmans, 1991), 526.
25. Morris, 684.
26. Laney, 289.

27. Laney, 290.
28. Laney, 290.
29. Laney, 292.
30. Bruce, F. F., *The Gospel and the Epistles of John.* (Grand Rapids, William B. Eerdmans Publishing Co., 1983), 324.
31. Morris, 711.
32. Musixmatch Songwriters: Rick Doyle Founds, *Lord, I Lift Your Name on High.* Lyrics © Universal Music – Brentwood Benson Publ.
33. Phillips, 315.
34. MacLaren, Alexander. *Expositions of Holy Scripture.* Published in 1904-1910; Public Domain, www.e-sword.net, note on John 16:32.

Suggested Books and Commentaries

<u>**The True Vine**</u> by Andrew Murray
<u>**Abide in Christ**</u> by Andrew Murray
<u>**Lessons from a Venetian Vinedresser**</u> by Robert Scott Stiner
<u>**In My Father's Vineyard**</u> by Wayne Jacobsen
<u>**The Farewell Discourse and Final Prayer of Jesus**</u> by D. A. Carson
<u>**Biblical Doctrine**</u> edited by John Macarthur and Richard Mayhue
<u>**The Moody Bible Commentary**</u> edited by Michael Rydelnik and Michael Vanlaningham
<u>**The Complete Word Study Dictionary**</u> by Spiros Zhodiates
<u>**The Strongest Strong's Exhaustive Concordance**</u> by James Strong — available through online resources below and Google

Suggested (free) online study helps:
These include various Bible translations and links to all resources mentioned below.

studylight.org   **searchgodsword.org**   **bliblehub.org**

e-sword.net (free program to download, then available offline)

The following list includes study helps that are available for free online if you are interested in pursuing more information about the Scriptures on your own. Descriptions are from e-sword.net.

Suggested downloads for E-sword:

Commentaries:
Robertson's Word Pictures in the New Testament
Robertson's magnum opus has a reputation as one of the best New Testament word study sets. Providing verse-by-verse commentary, it stresses meaningful and pictorial nuances implicit in the Greek but often lost in translation. And for those who do not know Greek, exegetical material and interpretive insights are directly connected with studies in the original text. All Greek words are transliterated.

Treasury of Scriptural Knowledge
This classic Bible study help gives you a concordance, chain-reference system, topical Bible and commentary all in one! Turn to any Bible passage, and you'll find chapter synopses, key word cross-references, topical references, parallel passages and illustrative notes that show how the Bible comments on itself. This really is a treasure!

Vincent's Word Studies
Marvin Vincent's Word Studies has been treasured by generations of pastors and laypeople. Commenting on the meaning, derivation, and uses of significant Greek words and idioms, Vincent helps you incorporate the riches of the New Testament in your sermons or personal study without spending hours on tedious language work!

John Gill's Exposition of the Entire Bible
Having preached in the same church as C. H. Spurgeon, John Gill is little known, but his works contain gems of information found nowhere outside of the ancient Jewish writings. John Gill presents a verse-by-verse exposition of the entire Bible.

Jamieson, Fausset and Brown Commentary
Long considered one of the best conservative commentaries on the entire Bible, the JFB Bible Commentary offers practical insight from a reformed evangelical perspective. The comments are an insightful balance between learning and devotion, with an emphasis on allowing the text to speak for itself.

Keil & Delitzsch Commentary on the Old Testament
This commentary is a classic in conservative biblical scholarship! Beginning with the nature and format of the Old Testament, this evangelical commentary examines historical and literary aspects of the text, as well as grammatical and philological issues. Hebrew words and grammar are used, but usually in content, so you can follow the train of thought.

Dictionaries:
Easton's Bible Dictionary
Easton's Bible Dictionary provides informative explanations of histories, people and customs of the Bible. An excellent and readily understandable source of information for the student and layperson. This dictionary is one of Matthew George Easton's most significant literary achievements.

International Standard Bible Encyclopedia
This authoritative reference dictionary explains every significant word in the Bible and Apocrypha! Learn about archaeological discoveries, the language and literature of Bible lands, customs, family life, occupations, and the historical and religious environments of Bible people.

Smith's Bible Dictionary
A classic reference, this comprehensive Bible dictionary gives you thousands of easy-to-understand definitions, verse references and provides a wealth of basic background information that you'll find indispensable as you read the Bible.

Thayer's Greek Definitions
For over a century, Joseph Henry Thayer's Greek-English Lexicon of the New Testament has been lauded as one of the finest available! Based on the acclaimed German lexicon by C.L.W. Grimm, Thayer's work adds comprehensive extra-biblical citations and etymological information, expanded references to other works, increased analysis of textual variations, and discussion of New Testament synonyms. An invaluable resource for students of New Testament Greek!

Noah Webster's Dictionary of American English
Noah Webster once wrote, "Education is useless without the Bible." That's why his first dictionary is the only one available today that defines every word in the original language and its biblical usage. Compare Webster's definitions of words like "marriage" and "education" with those found in modern dictionaries, and see the difference for yourself!

Today's date:

My personal request:

Confidential requests from my friends:

Today's date:

My personal request:

Confidential requests from my friends:

Today's date:

My personal request:

Confidential requests from my friends:

Today's date:

My personal request:

Confidential requests from my friends:

Today's date:

My personal request:

Confidential requests from my friends:

Prayer Requests and Praises

Today's date:

My personal request:

Confidential requests from my friends:

Today's date:

My personal request:

Confidential requests from my friends:

Today's date:

My personal request:

Confidential requests from my friends:

Prayer Requests and Praises

Today's date:

My personal request:

Confidential requests from my friends:

Today's date:

My personal request:

Confidential requests from my friends:

Today's date:

My personal request:

Confidential requests from my friends:

Prayer Requests and Praises

Today's date:

My personal request:

Confidential requests from my friends:

OTHER STUDIES BY ELIZABETH BAGWELL FICKEN

And the Lord Blessed Job: An in-depth Bible study of Job
One of the Lord's blessings to Job was that he was chosen to show Satan that God is worthy of worship no matter what happens in our lives. While the book of Job deals with suffering, it isn't about answering the question "why do people suffer?" It's about humbly submitting to God as the Holy One who is infinite in wisdom, power, justice, and goodness.

Come Let Us Worship: An in-depth Bible study of Psalms
The Psalms contain many of our most well-known Scriptures, offering comfort and expressing the emotions of our souls. They challenge us to godly living, always trusting the Lord. What a beautiful arrangement of poems, prayers, and praises God has given us! From Psalm 1 to Psalm 150, you'll study selected psalms in the order of their placement in the Scriptures.

That You May Know the Lord: An in-depth Bible study of Ezekiel
Don't miss this great book! As you study this intriguing prophecy, you will be humbled by the holiness, sovereignty and glory of God; you will be challenged to examine your own lives as you see the sin of the Israelites; you will be inspired as you see the power of the Holy Spirit; and you will be excited as you anticipate wonderful promises to be fulfilled by the Lord.

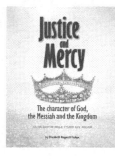
Justice and Mercy — The Character of God, the Messiah, and the Kingdom: An in-depth Bible study of Micah
Who is like God? The prophet Micah tells us! This short book of prophecy declares God's judgment against injustice which will prompt us to examine how we live our lives and treat others. It also declares God's overwhelming mercy to forgive sins. And it unveils the Lord's extraordinary plans for Israel during the Millennial Kingdom when Jesus Christ reigns supreme.

Follow Me: An in-depth Bible study of the Gospel of Matthew
This study will challenge you to a more passionate commitment to Jesus. Learn from Matthew's eye-witness perspective, his proofs from Old Testament scriptures, and his presentation of Jesus' five sermons, just who Jesus is, what He did, and what He said. Matthew's life was drastically changed from his encounter with Jesus—yours will be too.

Believe in Me — The Death and Resurrection of Jesus Christ: an in-depth study of Luke 22-24
Experience an eye-opening, gut-wrenching, faith-strengthening study of Luke's carefully researched account. You'll learn that Judas the traitor was influenced by Satan. That the disciples abandoned Jesus. That powerful people testified to Jesus' innocence. That Jesus was crucified and declared dead…. And that He rose from the dead! Jesus offers freedom from sin, a relationship with His holy Father, and an eternal life of joy.

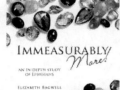
Immeasurably More!: An in-depth Bible study of Ephesians
Do you want your walk with Christ to be more intimate, more faithful, and more obedient? God is able to do immeasurably more than you can imagine through His power in your life! This exciting study will help you understand the never-ending blessings of salvation and the extraordinary potential you have to live a victorious and faithful Christian life.

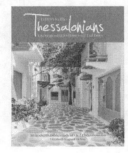
Letters to the Thessalonians — Encouragement for living in the End Times: An in-depth Bible study of 1st and 2nd Thessalonians
These letters are about faith, hope and love; holiness, prayer, and perseverance; the will of God and the glorious return of Christ. And so much more! Almost every major doctrine of our faith is covered in these personal writings from the apostle Paul. Join me as we read someone else's mail. I'm sure you'll find a few things that you will think were written just to you!

Hold Fast to Jesus: An in-depth Bible study of Hebrews
In this study of the personal, passionate letter of exhortation to "go on to maturity," we'll consider deep doctrines including the new covenant and atonement. We'll be warned not to drift away from our great salvation. We'll be encouraged to persevere through suffering as the great heroes of the faith did. We'll see that Jesus is our great High Priest who has provided what no other priest ever could. Let us fix our eyes on Jesus and hold fast to Him.

From the Author:
Thank you for studying the Bible with me! If you have enjoyed reading this book, please share a brief review on Amazon or on social media. You can help other readers decide whether to read the book too, and you can help spread the word of God!

Blessings, Elizabeth

Find her! elizabethficken.com or

Thank you for studying God's word with me!

It's been such a delight and privilege and plenty of hard work to write the Bible studies described on the previous pages.

Each is available on Amazon and at The Shepherd's Church bookstore.

Use the workbooks for:
Individual Bible study
Small group Bible study
Sunday School classes
Homeschooling

Visit elizabethficken.com for more resources

Free Videos:
30-45 minute lectures which supplement workbook lessons, including handouts and powerpoint presentations

Free leader's guides:
audio discussions of how to lead each workbook lesson

Find me on your favorite podcast apps:
In-depth Bible Study with Elizabeth Ficken

Find my lectures on YouTube:
In-depth Bible Studies
@elizabethficken

Made in the USA
Middletown, DE
19 October 2024

62908122R00062